MY NEAR DEATH EXPERIMENT

life-change by design instead of disaster

by Caleb Anderson

MyNearDeathExperiment.com

Published by CrossSection

940 Calle Negocio #175

San Clemente, CA 92673

800-946-5983

crosssection.com

Book + Jacket design by Crosssection

Set in Adobe Garamond & Gotham

First Edition: September 2013

Printed in the USA

ISBN 978-0-9847577-7-0 (paperback)

ISBN 978-0-9847577-8-7 (e-book)

My Near Death Experiment might be the awakening you need! This book is for anyone who knows that self-help needs a spiritual make-over, and that faith needs to stay grounded in practical life. Follow Caleb on this enlightening journey of life-change that matters!

—Chris Widener, author of The Art of Influence,
www.WidenerLeadership.com

Too many people live boring, unintentional lives—stuck in autopilot, or worse. My Near Death Experiment is a wake-up call, and an invitation to more. Caleb has developed an "experiment" that just might take you on a journey you never knew you always wanted.

—Mike Foster, Co-Founder of XXXChurch
and People of the Second Chance

My Near Death Experiment will make you stand up take action! Caleb reminds us of two certainties: We all die. And there is a Living God who created us to with purpose and meaning. So read this book and make the most of the life you've been given!

—Roger Sandberg, Humanitarian Aid Consultant,
Wheaton College Adjunct Faculty

Who among us doesn't wish for more perspective in life circumstances, and for the ability to get the most out of what life has to offer? Caleb offers a way for us to do just that.

—Cary Paine, Executive Director,
The Stewardship Foundation

My Near Death Experiment is piercing, profound, and practical. Caleb Anderson's book is a must-read for anyone seeking clarity in their calling or looking to break free from the chains of apathy.

—Albus Brooks, City Councilman, Denver, CO

Life is short; don't wait another minute before reading Caleb's life-changing book! You will live more fully and love more deeply as a result.

—Peter Greer, President and CEO, HOPE International
and author of The Spiritual Danger of Doing Good

Reading My Near Death Experiment is a gentle, courageous guide into truth delivered with humility which always equals wisdom. Read and Do. This book will help direct the journey of a life well-lived. My highest recommendation!

  —Marty Caldwell, Sr. VP, Young Life

My Near Death Experiment takes the concept of life purpose and makes it approachable to any reader. Caleb's pragmatic, wisdom-laden approach readily resonates and motivates any reader and perhaps more importantly provides a path to taking action so that anyone can improve the quality of their life.

  —David Roberts, President & CEO, The Billing Tree

We loved doing the Near Death Experiment! Part of it was the novelty and arresting concept... But most of it had to do with the spirit of Jesus that Caleb's material was enveloped in. It's not a gimmick or a quick fix. The Near Death Experiment is a thoughtful but provocative opportunity to present eternity to people captivated by the present. In a world imprisoned with the "tyranny of the urgent," this concept is refreshing and significant. I love Caleb and I love the work he's done here. Buy it, use it, live it.

  —Dean Curry, Sr. Pastor, Life Center Tacoma

"The most compelling people are the most committed, with nothing left to lose." So says, Caleb Anderson in his most helpful book. All of us need to live with more intentionality. We need a sense of urgency for the important parts of life. Caleb has given the church a wonderful tool and resource to do just this. I highly recommend My Near Death Experience for your church.

  —Dr. Larry Anderson, Sr. Pastor, North Bible Church

To Hilary,

My not-so-secret weapon...

Your love inspires me.

Your heart amazes me.

Your genius empowers me.

I am lucky,

And I am grateful.

And, to Kimi...

Your life echoes.

TABLE OF CONTENTS

Change is going to happen with or without you.

We are all humans becoming

ORIGINS

"Remembering you are going to die is the best way I know to avoid the trap of thinking you have something to lose."
—Steve Jobs

BY WAY OF INTRODUCTION

"Men, this is a football."
—Vince Lombardi

Vince Lombardi was arguably the greatest football coach in NFL history. But that didn't mean he always won. In fact, Lombardi—a stickler for the fundamentals—once addressed his team in the locker room at halftime of a game they were significantly down in points. "Men, this is a football."

In other words, "We need to start over--get back to the basics. You think you're impressive professional football players, but you're not doing the simple things—the fundamentals—that win games."

You can be 16 or 86… You can be a PhD or high school drop-out… A millionaire or a struggling musician. It doesn't matter. There are fundamentals of a life-well lived. Fundamentals that are easy to forget, miss, or ignore.

Whether you're just starting out, at halftime, or nearing the end, *My Near Death Experiment* is a wake-up call. Consider it your locker room pep-talk.

"Friend. This is your life. And you only get one. Make the most of it."

* * *

The concept of *My Near Death Experiment* began as a catchy way to inspire young adults to make positive changes in their lives. It began in a particular place at a particular time. And it worked. Starting with a thousand college students at a major university, people were intrigued and inspired. Our group increased in numbers; participants shared their thoughts, regrets, decisions, and intentions on a community blog. And there was significant buzz around the university community. But it became much bigger than that…and much more personal, at the same time.

Bigger because more groups, more people, and more places heard about what we were doing and wanted to facilitate their own version of the campaign. These, by the way, have been everything from families, support groups, community organizations, churches, businesses, and schools.

And yet, as the momentum grew, the concept simultaneously became more intimate in my own life.

Shortly after the original Near Death Experiment campaign, my wife, Hilary, got a phone call that would change our lives. It was her mom. Her mom was her best friend. They talked everyday of her life—often multiple times.

Ten years prior, her mom had overcome a bout with breast cancer. The tone in her mom's voice reminded Hilary of that painful time.

"I've got some bad news, Sweetie."

"No…what is it mama?"

"It looks like the cancer's back."

"No mama! Please, no…" I watched helplessly as my precious wife of three months became a younger child, desperately reaching out for her mother to give her hope.

"It looks like it's worse this time, Hilary. It's not a good cancer."

"God, please…No, mama…Are they sure? I'm on my way."

And she was. She was on a flight a few hours later. She slept the next night with her mom in the hospital bed.

I stayed behind, working and trying to figure out what all this would mean. I was in the middle of things—work and other obligations. We still had rent to pay, money invested, and goals to pursue. In reality, I was partly responsible, partly selfish. But it quickly became clear that this would be a matter of life and death.

I remember the night, alone in our apartment, the reality of the situation hit home for me. I was reading Hilary's heart-wrenching daily posts regarding Kimi's health and outlook on the CaringBridge.org blog. Then she called me and I listened to my wife's quivering voice as she asked why this was happening to her sweet Kimi. And I realized that I was in the wrong place.

I packed a couple bags and started driving the next morning. I pulled over in a Costco parking lot in Northern California and slept in the front seat for four hours then kept driving. I arrived at the Franciscan Hospital in Tacoma, WA later that evening. This was the same hospital that Kimi had worked for 30 years. She had managed 150 staff, many of whom had become like family. And several of whom were now monitoring Kimi as she fought for life in her fourth stage of Pancreatic Cancer.

Despite a valiant fight, Kimi lost her battle with pancreatic cancer on July 8, 2009.

Over 1,000 people turned out for Kimi's funeral. Hers was a life well-lived. And yet it was Kimi's *death* that became a turning point for my own life.

Hilary and I had left our home, family, and friends to be at Kimi's bedside, and we never returned to our old life. I count it one of my greatest privileges—being present in those last days; helping to escort Kimi to the gate of the Great Transition. And then to watch her family's expression of love. I watched my young wife hold her mom's head for the last breaths of life. I joined the immediate family around a bedside with no answers, just presence.

My previous training as a minister seemed almost useless. My gifts of wisdom and insight abandoned me. And yet I wondered if I'd ever been closer to God.

The morning after Kimi died I began to journal. My life felt different. My successes seemed less significant. My failures seemed less final. Every single morning for the next year I wrote down in my journal things I was thankful for. After all, I was alive.

*   *   *

The Near Death Experiment became *My* Near Death Experiment. I was intimately acquainted with tragedy and the brevity of our lives. It was no longer a concept or a message to help someone else—confused college students, or others who needed direction or inspiration. No. It was about me. I wanted to change. I wanted to experience a more full and free way of life. I wanted to love others better.

The image and reputation I used to care so much about began collecting dust as I put on a new man that felt strangely original. I began to care less and less about what people thought, and I began to dream again. My eyes were opened, and I could see my relationships as gifts instead of leveraging them or comparing myself. I established patterns that led toward intentional growth and progress. I had an increasing desire to care for my own health. I genuinely wanted to make the most of what I'd been given.

I grew up with the notion that my life would have an ongoing "up-and-to-the-right" trajectory, like the graphs and charts every business owner wants to see—growth, progress, profits! And, I assumed, that if I did all the right things, life would get better and better: pleasure and profits on the rise, pain at a minimum.

But it turns out, that's crap. You might just have to lose your life to find it.[1] You might have to find out the hard way that life is precious. You might have to look death in the eye to have your life transformed.

Or, you might be able to learn from the experiences of others who have come before you…others whose lives have been changed…others who are living their dream…and who choose a life well-lived.

If you're desperate to reach your potential, this book has a message for you. If you're interested in making changes in your life—for the first time or the 1,000th time—this book can help. If you think your life is fine and you just need some refining, refocusing, or inspiration, these pages will take you further.

*   *   *

---

1.   *Luke 9:24*

Have you ever thought about why the greatest athletes, actors, musicians, and executives in the world have coaches? Most of them are being coached by someone who themselves, never reached the level of performance as their coaching client. Why would a giant in his or her profession ask someone else for help?

It's because *everybody needs a nudge.*

Once in a while, we all get stuck. We all have blind spots that cause us to miss certain things. We all fall into life-as-usual ruts, and we need someone outside of our own heads to help us spark change.

Let *My Near Death Experiment* be your nudge. You might have your act together. People might look at you and think you're on top of the world. But you picked up this book for a reason.

There's an ancient proverb that says, "When the student is ready, the teacher will appear." I believe that there is something in your life that is about to change. I am convinced that you are reading this book because it's time for you to take the next step in your journey--whether you realize it yet or not. I don't know what that means for you, but soon, *you* will know. And I hope to help you take the next leap toward living a more full, intentional, and healthy life.

I've also recruited others for this book that you can learn from. I've studied and interviewed countless people who've overcome adversities, lived through tragedy, achieved the exceptional, or become someone respectable. A number of their stories are referenced in these pages.

Use this book as a tool. If possible, read it along with others. Not necessarily out-loud, kindergarten-style, but perhaps together at the same time—like in a group or with friends or family. Relationships make our worlds go 'round.

God bless you on this journey. Welcome to *My Near Death Experiment.*

Remember, book is only part of the *Experiment.* You can engage on a number of levels. *Your Near Death Experiment* can be as simple and/or significant as you choose.

Visit **MyNearDeathExperiment.com** for videos, resources, tools, and connections. Use whatever serves you, however it best fits you.

BY WAY OF ORGANIZATION

My Near Death Experiment is broken up into small chapters. Big ideas; bite-sized dosages; room to breathe. Personally, I appreciate books that give me the option to pause and put it down every ten minutes—even if I have the time or passion to read it straight through.

It's been said that to break a habit we need to replace the old habit with a new habit. And that process requires at least 30 days of momentum to take hold. This book was designed to give you the opportunity to engage it over 30+ days, if you so choose.

The ideas in this book might challenge some of your thinking and beliefs, but the goal is to move you to action. Ideas that don't lead to action are useless.

My mentor, Kenton Beshore, concludes most meetings by asking the newer or younger members of his team, "What did you see, what did you learn?" In other words, don't just show up. Get something out of this time. Don't just read a book. Learn something and change something about your life.

At the end of every reading you'll find a Question and an Action step. They are part of your Experiment. Make them work for you. Apply your learnings.

Then, at the end of this book you'll find a Death Contract. This is an opportunity for you to do business with death—deciding to live each day with renewed passion and intentionality…leveraging the lessons and cementing a few as new habits.

My Near Death Experiment is not meant to be prescriptive. It is designed to expose subtle lies, promote truth, and create space for ideas and actions to shape the life of your choosing. Take and apply whatever serves you.

Be bold. Be courageous. Make the most of this experience.

Here's to a life of peace, purpose, and passion…

Why do I keep saying, "Tomorrow, tomorrow"? Why not today?

A WAKE

"I'm not yet desperate enough to do anything about the conditions that are making me desperate."
—Ashleigh Brilliant

MEET JOE DEATH

"You and I were born with an expiration date."
–Erwin W. Lutzer

You only live once. That's not a pass to be reckless or irresponsible. It's a reminder.

There was a popular song not long ago called "Live Like You Were Dying." That seems like a good idea. I mean, if I actually believed I was going to die at the end of the day today I'd likely live a little differently. I'd call some people, write some things down, spend time with my family, and I'd consider what it means to prepare my soul to meet God.

Yet even now, as I try, I can't conjure up the emotion of a death sentence, or a cancer report, or a car accident. In this moment, my imagination doesn't take me there. I can cognitively agree that the day is coming, but I don't feel the emotional sense of urgency. Not now. Not yet. And that's why I've written this book. I hope to give you glimpses of death—physical and metaphorical—for the sake of elevating life. A little dose of death can lead to a new level of living. Stick with me…

* * *

Death has a lesson for you.

I know—you'd rather not think about death. We like to pretend. We pride ourselves in delaying the inevitable reality, and even dismissing the effects of aging wherever possible. We prefer to ignore our ultimate fate. But in doing so we numb some part of ourselves.

You cannot live your life with fullness, clarity, and purpose until you have made a strategic arrangement with death.

Mike was about to live his dream. He had finally gotten out of Ohio and had made it to the West Coast. He had big plans for work and school, making progress toward a life that once seemed like wishful thinking. But now it was happening. Until he got the call.

His father had been sick for awhile but the cancer had fatally progressed and he was given nine months to live. The reality of his father's life-cut-short crystalized a new perspective in Mike's mind. He hung up the phone, packed up his apartment, and moved back to his family's home in Ohio. Without debate or deliberation Mike's priorities were redefined—his utmost values emerged and difficult decision-making was simple, automatic.

When you come face-to-face with death, what matters most in life becomes more clear.

Returning home, Mike took care of his mom and younger sister. He sat with his father, talked about life, love, and sports. Mike lovingly and patiently escorted his father to the gates of heaven. He counts it as the most significant season of his life.

And then there's Beth. Beth was returning from her senior trip. It had been six days of partying in Mexico. She didn't want to go home. Her relationship with her parents was strained. She wanted more freedom. With her parents going through a divorce, Beth was disillusioned with family, responsibility, and commitments. She was preparing to tell her parents that she would forego her scholarship at a small private school in the Northwest and move to San Diego with some friends she'd met on the senior trip.

Beth joined her friends for one last night of partying before they caught the red-eye flight home. Beth doesn't have full recollection of the events of the evening, but she knows that she was jumped by two men in the restroom of the club. Details are not necessary here, but Beth was beaten and abused. She woke up in a strange hospital room to a frenzy of Spanish-speaking nurses. When she stabilized a day later, she woke up to find both of her parents there with her. They wept together over her pain, but the tears quickly turned to joy, as her precious life was spared. There was more for her.

Drifting in and out of consciousness, Beth says that she caught a glimpse of the other side—of heaven. "I think I saw heaven. I wasn't sure, but I felt lucky to be going there. Then I got this sense like there was more for me on earth. And I woke up, and that was it."

That event changed everything for Beth. Not because she was scarred or damaged. Actually, quite the opposite. She was hurt, but in tact. The incident gave her a whole new perspective on her life. She saw clearly that her life had great value.

Beth went to her school in the Northwest. She lived with a sense of urgency, understanding that her life was spared. She embraced forgiveness. She took on leadership, becoming the president of a group on campus that educated women on staying safe and elevating their self-esteem. She woke up to a life of meaning.

* * *

Near-death in *proximity* can change you.

In 1994, almost 1,000,000 people were murdered in the Rwandan genocide in East Africa (almost 20% of the country's population). It was the culmination of longstanding ethnic tensions between the minority Tutsi tribe, who had controlled power for centuries, and the majority Hutu peoples, who had come to power in the rebellion of 1959–62. The killing went on for some 100 days. Neighbors killed neighbors. Family members turned on one another. It was unimaginable chaos and human depravity.

Those 100 days have forever changed the country. Rwanda—known as "The Land of 1,000 Hills"—is beautiful in nature, but carries with it scars and the heavy burden of its brutal past.

Twelve years after the genocide, I visited Rwanda. I visited the famous memorial of the genocide. The images, the bones, the stories, the facts… It was too much. My mind couldn't fathom the experience of the people. Nor could I imagine how now, today, they were living side-by-side once again—trying to forgive and put the pain of the past behind them. I realized that I spend most of my life trying to avoid thinking about death and tragedy. But, sometimes, proximity to death can haunt you into appreciating your life.

Proximity to pain, loss, and death usually has one of three effects on someone:

1. **Paralysis:** Becoming numb or frozen because of the shock—not sure how to respond, what to feel, or what to do.

2. **Bitterness:** Going negative and developing a skeptical, jaded outlook, because death often produces fear, confusion, and meaninglessness.

3. **Passion:** Turning bad into good…looking for the hope amidst the pain…and choosing to live your life with a sense of urgency, knowing how quickly things can change.

My Near Death Experiment is an opportunity to leverage death and pain for the sake of passion. When death comes near, perspective sharpens. Life is illuminated. Time slows down.

The greatest athletes have claimed to reach a level of focus and devotion to their sport such that the "game slows down" and their minds make decisions, perceive opportunities, and execute desired outcomes with relative ease and efficiency. Similarly, close proximity to death has a way of focusing our senses, eliminating distractions, and calling out the most passionate parts of us.

Death is not a future to be feared, but a reality to be leveraged.

Like Beth and Mike, you, too can wake up to the things that matter most in life.

Experiment

Question:

What death or loss has had the most profound impact on you? What have you believed or become as a result?

Action:

Schedule time for Your Near Death Experiment. Time to read and reflect. Now text someone else and tell them about your plan. It will help you carry it out.

HOW TO BE INSPIRED

"Change comes from inspiration or desperation."
-Jim Rohn

You have everything you need.

Your future, your passion, your joy, your contentment, your success, and your growth are not a matter of circumstance or happenstance. They will not be realized by reaching some other place, platform, or status in life. Neither are they determined by your talent or even will power.

You have what you need when you awaken *inspiration.*

My own definitions...

Motivation: Trying to get someone moving from the outside

Inspiration: Drawing out something of significance from inside a person

Semantics? Perhaps. But there's a reason why I think the distinction matters. It's the difference between pressures and passions.

An angry boss might motivate you by applying pressure. He'll try and cause you to behave in certain ways by leveraging the fear of pain or punishment. "If you don't reach your commission goals this month you'll be fired." Now, an ultimatum like that will certainly motivate a lot of people. But it also creates resentment, a lack of trust, and a culture of fear. There's a lack of teamwork in environments like that. And there is also a lack of true passion. You're not working hard because you love what you're doing and love why you're doing it. Instead, you're operating out of fear of punishment.

I don't want you to be afraid of dying. I want to offer you opportunities to tap into things that inspire you, and to awaken a renewed passion for living.

As you'll see, we're going to continue to leverage death and failure for the sake of more life. Death, perceived death, failure, and disappointment are common to all human beings. Don't fear or hide from these realities. Use them! Use them to learn. Use them to spark passion for living better—a life increasingly free of doubt, fear, and insecurity.

If you look throughout history, those who have added the most to our society and to our personal lives did so *in spite* of circumstances, not because of them.

Many of the most inspiring people in the world have suffered great loss before offering their greatest gifts. And so, even their suffering becomes a gift…to you.

Steve Jobs was fired by Apple—his own company. The devastating rejection led to an awakening for Jobs. He started a new company that would later be bought by Apple. Once re-instated as president, he turned Apple around, making it (around the time of his death) the most valuable company in the world.

Abraham Lincoln suffered through the death of loved ones and numerous failed campaigns before being elected the 16th President of the United States. His legacy of unlikely triumph is among the great stories in American history.

Rick Warren had a nervous breakdown when he started what would become one of the most influential churches in American history. And after enduring two decades of criticism for his methods, he wrote the best-selling non-fiction hardback book of its kind, *The Purpose-Driven Life*.

J.K. Rowling was literally homeless. After writing the Harry Potter series, she became wealthier than the Queen of England.

Dave Ramsey had a financial near-death experience, filing for bankruptcy and losing everything, before he dedicated his life to helping others avoid the mistakes that he himself had made.

Megan was in a motorcycle accident where she was paralyzed from the chest down. "Ironically," she says, "I hated my life *before* my accident. I was lonely and angry. Now I appreciate each day. Not being able to walk has slowed me down enough to see that life is beautiful." Megan got a scholarship to the University of Illinois for wheelchair basketball. She kayaks competitively and gives inspirational speeches to children with disabilities.

Countless people living exceptional lives are doing so leveraging experiences you and I can learn from, especially disappointment and tragedy. Some had near-death experiences themselves. Others were near death in proximity. Still others have suffered failure, betrayals, hurts, and disappointment—all helping to fuel a passion to live this new day to the fullest.

Pain can be converted to passion and new perspective. And get this: It doesn't even have to be your own pain! You can spare yourself the regrets, scars, and wasted time. Or, you can ignore the warnings until you feel the sting yourself.

I grew up hearing that wisdom comes from experience. A wise person has experiences—good and bad—learns from them, and thus becomes wise. That's true. And incomplete.

The wisest people learn not only from their own experiences, but also from the experiences of others. Wisdom learns. Wisdom observes. Wisdom receives.

You can choose to use the pain and perspective of others as inspiration for your own journey. You can increase the intensity of how you feel about the lessons you care to learn. You can leverage this book, this moment, and make it work for you. You can change your life for the good without having to go through all the bad.

Experiment

Question:

What lessons have you learned from the lives of others? What inspiration or idea has already struck you at the start of this book?

Action:

Cultivate inspiration. Every morning this week, read something that sparks inspiration in you. Watch a video on Ted.com. Pray for passion. Remind yourself of things that are true.

SIGNIFICANT LEARNING MOMENT

Significant Learning Moment (SLM): To receive and apply some lesson in life from the wisdom of another, without having to go through a memorable life experience. **Significant Life Experience (SLE):** To learn through a life-shaping event.

By now, I hope you're on board with this statement: Wisdom comes from experience; but the purest wisdom is in learning from the experience of others. The saddest and most destructive and disastrous lives are those whose paths are marked by a complete lack of wisdom. These people wander aimlessly, live purposelessly, and blame God or others for their disastrous journeys. They are the foolish.

Foolishness: To learn neither from the wisdom of others, nor from the circumstances and consequences of one's own life choices.

Now, all of us are foolish at times. But foolish as a pattern is something else altogether.

Someone said that the definition of insanity is to do the same thing over and over again and expect a different result. But that's not what you and I do. We're not insane—we know the results. Yet sometimes, with certain issues, we do the same thing over and over again because we like the *immediate* result. Though wisdom suggests that the long-term effect will be negative, we keep doing the thing because of the quick-fix feeling it gives us. In fact, we'll manage our little addiction, ignoring the Significant Learning Moments along the way until we ultimately encounter some Significant Life Event that gets our attention. Perhaps it's diabetes. Maybe your spouse leaves or the bank takes your house. Whatever the situation, it's messy, and the splatter stains others, too, not just you.

After only a few months working at my first real job out of college, I was late to a big staff meeting. I was driving from my apartment, 30 minutes away, or 20 minutes by Toll Road. I was still trying to prove my value to the organization and I didn't want to be late, so I took the toll road. I think it was $2.25. I was heading N/E on the 133, driving a smooth 85. I was in the left lane, heavy-footed, considering in my mind which door I would enter at the office to attract the least amount of attention. I came up on a forest green Ford Expedition, probably cruising along at 65 mph in the right lane. As I pulled within 10 feet of it I recognized the bumper sticker in the rear window. "Why do I know that sticker," I thought to myself?

I was going 20 mph faster than the SUV with the sticker, but I let off the gas and looked in the driver's window as I passed. First, I saw a right hand waiving. Then I saw a genuine smile. Then… I realize it was my boss, Rick Warren. He was late for his own staff meeting, and yet he was driving the speed limit. I knew he saw me, but did he recognize me? He might actually just waive and smile at everyone who blows by him on the freeway. He's a pastor. (And that's *so* "purpose-driven.")

I got about 50 yards in front of Rick's car, pulled into the right lane, and I slowed down to 70 mph. Slowing all the way to 65 felt inauthentic.

I beat him to the meeting. The chief of staff was leading the meeting and there were 200 other people in seats. No one noticed or cared that I was late. I sped, paid the toll, and flew by my boss for nothing. I felt a little silly, but that's about all.

When the meeting ended, I turned and was talking to a couple co-workers. All of the sudden, I felt a large arm around my shoulders, steering me just far enough from my conversation that the other two couldn't hear his whisper. It was Rick.

"Long time no see," he said with a father's voice and boyish twinkle in his eye. Then he walked away.

Keep in mind, please, that this man is the author of the best-selling non-fiction hardback book in the history of the world. Also, please remember that I was fresh out of college, in my first real job, and had dreams of following in the footsteps of this man.

That's why, for me, this silly situation became a Significant Learning Moment. It was a SLM for the following reasons:

- It was Rick Warren, and I looked up to him
- I was embarrassed, but he didn't embarrass me
- He was the busiest man I knew, yet he wasn't in a hurry
- He cared enough to make it a teachable moment for me

I've heard my dad and others talk about teachable moments when coaching younger parents. (There must've have been a book about that concept in the 80's.) The idea is that parents—or authority figures—be ready to turn a child's bad decision into an opportunity to learn. So, say, instead of immediately freaking out and spanking the bare booty, a parent might pull their child aside and explain the consequences of a course of action. (Then smack that backside.)

For instance, it's better for a child to learn that the stove is hot with mom right there than later with a distracted babysitter on their phone with her boyfriend ignoring the boiling pot of blue-box macaroni and cheese.

What was a "teachable moment" as a child becomes a Significant Learning Moment as an adult, but now it's up to us to receive and apply the learning—without the threat of a spanking.

So choose the SLM. Choose to receive and apply wisdom now, before the event—before the disaster.

Life can be difficult enough without participating in our own destruction. People in your life will die. Others willingly leave. There are natural disasters, freak accidents, and corporate down-sizing. So much of life is out of your control. But one thing is completely up to you: your choices.

You're choosing now. You're choosing what to do with what you're reading. You're choosing what you think of yourself—what you expect of your future. You might be racking your brain for reasons to put down this book and reach for a safe distraction. It's never easy to address the things in life that really matter. But it's better to do it now, with a little inspiration, than to have to learn from your own negative life event.

Experiment

Question:
Think of a time when you received and applied someone's wisdom. What pain might that SLM have saved you?

Action:
Write down one SLE and one SLM that you have lived or witnessed first-hand.

Now, go to **MyNearDeathExperiment.com/SLM** and share your lessons with others.

Can a man scoop fire into his lap without his clothes being burned? Can a man walk on hot coals without his feet being scorched?
—Proverbs 6:27-28

SLEEPWALKING

The African culture is much more comfortable with the idea of death than Western cultures. They also have strange superstitions related to death.

I'm writing this in the middle of the night in the Nairobi airport. I have another hour before our plane boards for Turkey. My international electrical plug-in adaptor is effectively keeping my MacBook juiced, and being that my internal clock doesn't know which way is up, I'm wide awake at 2 AM. I'm sitting on the floor to have access to the outlet; laptop on my thighs, glasses on, my legs extended, and back against the wall, surrounded by about 150 chairs filling the center of the room, most of them propping up half-asleep travelers.

In the past hour as I've sat here, I've had four or five Africans come up to my extended legs, pause, and say, "excuse me." With my long legs stretching to the base of the chair in front of me there's little room to step around. However, it's not like I'm blocking a major thoroughfare either. And this room is crawling with people. Plus, we're in Africa, not Germany. If someone is choosing to take this route to a chair or open piece of carpet, that's fine, but kindly step over my legs. I'm writing here.

After the fifth African paused and waited for me pull my legs to my chest for their clear passage, a friendly African woman adjacent to me said with a disarming smile: "Do you know why they don't walk over your legs?"

"No, I've been wondering."

"It's superstition. In Africa, we grew up believing that if you step over someone's legs it takes years off your life. That's why they wait for you to move them."

Well, that makes sense. The superstition doesn't make sense, but the strange pre-flight behavior does. I pulled my legs in—"Indian style"—and kept working.

* * *

You might not think of yourself as superstitious, but you have beliefs that are controlling your mind and limiting your experience of life.

Our subconscious mind runs our lives. More than 95% of what you do and don't do on a daily basis is the result of your subconscious mind. The subconscious stores a lifetime of data, desire, and experience. It reminds you what you believe about everything. It is the "default" that keeps you acting they way you act. The subconscious is like an engine that keeps up your routines, your patterns, and the basis for how you have trained yourself to behave.

If 95% of life is dictated by routine and the subconscious, then less than 5% of your experience is your conscious mind. Your conscious mind takes information in and evaluates it based on the input of your subconscious. In essence, you live most of your life in autopilot.

The fact of the matter is, we don't notice very much of our lives. For most of us, life in autopilot is boring, monotonous, and leading us in a direction we're not-so-sure about.

I worked with a woman who wanted to kick her coffee habit. Every time she passed her caffeine-experience dealer it was as if a tractor beam pulled her in. She had a latte habit that cost her the equivalent of a car payment.

She tried will-power, but her love of the bean was too strong. I suggested a new idea. I encouraged her to pay close attention.

"Notice everything you can about the moment you are drawn to the store. What are you wearing? Who are in your mirrors? Who's in front of the store? Who's in line? What does it look like they are doing today? Does it seem like the staff are having good days? Do you know their names? Is there anything unusual going on? Now, why is it that you want this coffee right now?"

The key for this woman was not that she quit coffee cold turkey. The key was that she saw that she was in control of her life and her decisions. And one way to begin to have that sense is to be fully in the present moment. Notice everything around you—and then what's going on *inside* you.

By beginning to notice, we can take steps toward retraining our subconscious mind instead of just being blindly led by it. By intentionally noticing, you experience a richer sense of being alive.

The second step is asking "why?" Why do I want this? Why do I feel that? Why am I sluggish? What makes me believe what I'm believing?

To change your behavior you have to understand your behavior. Then, you must begin to change your mind—your way of thinking. There is a thought or belief at the root of every behavior. The reason you haven't changed already is because of your beliefs, not your will power. Will power is not your problem. Throughout this Experiment, you will uncover beliefs and commitments that are serving you and others that are causing you to stumble. You'll uncover aspects of your life that you haven't been paying attention to…and other ways of living that are occupying far too much of your time.

But for now, wake up. Notice what's really happening. Begin to expose patterns that might be preventing your experience of a fuller life.

Experiment

Question:
What comes to mind when you think about your life in autopilot?

Action:
Notice your behaviors today. Notice what you do and say that is just pure routine and subconscious ritual. Write down the patterns that are serving you and routines that might be hurting you.

KILLING DEATH SOFTLY

"If you have to kill a snake, kill it once and for all."
—Japanese Proverb

There is manual of the United States Government Peace Corps used by its volunteers assigned to South America. In this manual is a page I found quite amusing. It was added to the manual specifically for those volunteers serving in the vast Amazon River jungles. The page explains exactly…

What To Do If Attacked By An Anaconda:

The anaconda is the largest snake in the world. It is a relative of the Boa Constrictor. It grows to 35 feet in length and weighs between three and four hundred pounds. If you are attacked by an Anaconda…

1. Do not panic. Do not run. The snake is faster than you are.
2. Lie flat on the ground.
3. Put your arms tight at your sides and your legs tight against one another.
4. Expect the snake to nudge and climb over your body.
5. Do not panic.
6. Allow the snake to examine you and begin to swallow you from the feet end.

7. Continue to lie perfectly still. The snake will begin to suck your legs into its body. This will take a long time.

8. Reach for your knife—stealthily. When the snake has reached your knees, slowly, and with as little movement as possible, reach down, take your knife, and gently slide it into the side of the snake's mouth, between the edge of its mouth and your leg. Then, quickly and forcefully, rip upwards, severing the snake's head.

9. Be sure your knife is sharp.

10. Be sure you have your knife.

I'll understand if you want to tear this page out of this book and keep it on your person, because…you never know.

In the world, you will have trouble[1]. You will face incredible challenges in your life—frightening, consuming, perhaps paralyzing circumstances…and you need to be ready. You need to have your knife, and it needs to be sharp. You're going to need to kill some things before the things kill you.

Let Your Near Death Experiment help you sharpen your knife. But, even with a sharp knife, you're going to have to choose what needs to die. And you're going to have to kill whatever needs to die before it kills you.

In parts of the Developing World, especially in times of drought, there are churches that practice an unusual form of baptism. When water is scarce, they dig a hole. The spiritual leader and the person getting "baptized" descend into a four-to-six-foot ditch. They say something about being buried with Jesus in His death, and then lay the person down, as if dead, only to rise again into newness of life—a metaphoric resurrection. It's a dry baptism…a death baptism.

What they are saying in that symbolic action is that their old life of selfishness and rebellion towards God is over. Their new life in relationship with God is beginning. The metaphoric death leads to new life.

If you want to live, some things are going to have to die. If you want to live your life to the fullest, you're going to have to kill something that keeps you empty. If you want to live big, you're going to have kill that which keeps life small. If you want to come more fully to life, you're going to have to deal with the matter of death.

In the pages that follow, we'll discuss various tools that will help you keep your knife sharp—to cut through the fluff, distraction, and discouragement of life. An unintentional life will make you dull. You have to choose to be sharp, healthy, and focused.

---

1. *John 16:33*

Remember:
1. Never panic
2. Keep your knife sharp
3. Be willing to kill things before they kill you

Experiment

Question:
What do you already know is threatening your life and health? What are you willing to do about it?

Action:
List three activities that help keep you sharp—focused, energized, healthy.

Examples:
*   Reading and journaling
*   Daily exercise
*   Meeting with a mentor

12-YEAR-OLD MENTOR

"Take control of your consistent emotions and begin to consciously and deliberately reshape your daily experience of life."
—Tony Robbins

I got to know Russ through my friend, Eric Boles, while working with his corporate training company. During the preliminary consulting meetings, we met with the key leaders of Russ's company, and Russ's name kept coming up. People referred to him as "the heart of this company." One senior leader said that Russ embodied the desired culture better than anyone else. High praise. I wanted to meet to the guy.

Russ did not disappoint. He was even more inspiring and his positive outlook even more infectious than the Russ I had imagined in my head. I just had to ask...

"Russ, you're a remarkable human being. Your co-workers love you; the leadership of your organization appreciates you; and I'm already a fan! What is it? What drives you? How is it that you're the way you are?"

"Well," Russ answered, "I had a special mentor."

"Really? Tell me about him."

"I wasn't always as passionate about life as what you see today. Actually, I used to be a complete grump. A selfish man who hated my life. And rightly so, I thought, given the hand I was dealt.

I got married young. My wife and I were in love. We were looking forward to a long, full life together. But shortly after our first anniversary, she was killed in a car accident."

Gasp. "I'm so sorry."

"I spiraled into a deep depression. I kept working, but other than that, I pretty much checked out of life. I thought God hated me. I had lost the love of my life, and I didn't think I'd ever find anyone else again. It was several years before I seriously dated another woman. And it was several more years before I married her. I was so scared of losing the one I loved that I tried to convince myself I didn't really love her. Looking back, I was lucky she was willing to marry me, because I was still pretty detached and stuck in my own mind.

"Then, naturally, she wanted to have a children. And, again, I was in self-protection mode. The idea of loving a child that could be snatched from my grasp was a big deal for me. I dragged my feet for another couple years before conceding. Our beautiful baby girl was born two month premature and had significant complications. I had that awful feeling inside—that she wasn't going to make it. Our precious baby girl never left the hospital. She died a week after she was born. My wife and I were devastated. But for me, this was proof that my life was cursed. God obviously hated me, so I hated God, and myself, and my life.

"I tolerated my wife, but pulled away more and more. I completely expected her to leave or to die tragically anyway. She wanted to have another child, but I refused. I was cursed. Why would we bring that curse upon ourselves or another child? Besides, it felt like my heart had grown cold and I was losing my capacity to love.

"We did get pregnant, however. And I resented it. I felt manipulated. I wasn't ready. I didn't care to be a dad. I was barely a husband.

"I barely held our son after he was born. I can't imagine how it must've made my wife feel. But, at the time, I didn't care. I was convinced he'd be ripped from our grasp.

"A year went by, and he was alive and well. Then two years. And five years. I slowly began to wonder if the curse on my life was somehow lifted. My wife assured me there was no curse and I started to believe her. I began to allow myself to love and care for my family. I became more affectionate with my wife. And I paid attention to my son. It was a slow progression, but by the time he was ten years old, I was almost a normal, engaged, soccer-coaching dad. Then, when my son turned ten years old, it happened. At first, we thought it was a normal illness, but it got worse. When we took him to the doctor they ordered a bunch of tests. My heart sunk. I assumed the worse.

"Even before my precious boy was diagnosed with leukemia I was already beginning to pull away again. It was exactly what I was afraid of. This was the story of my life. My life was cursed and that curse would kill my son, too. I thought, 'who could lose the three people closest to them and not hate life itself?' So I checked out. I considered suicide but didn't go through with it. Instead, I just let myself die from the inside.

"My son lived for two more years, but in my mind he was already dead. I went to work, came home, ignored him and my wife, watched television, and went to bed. The longer I behaved that way, the more his little heart broke. I remember it like it was yesterday.

"I remember walking in the door from work, having eaten fast food on my way home. My wife asked me if I wanted to join them for dinner. I declined with a noise—not even looking at her. I sat down in my usual spot on the couch and turned on the television. After a few minutes, I could literally feel the presence of my weakened son. He was standing to my left, staring at me. I let him stand there for several moments before I finally looked over. He was shaking. His eyes were wide and red. Tears were streaming down his face. He had reached his emotional breaking point. I felt my heart seize up, but I turned my head instead of acknowledging the pain I was causing. Then, in a voice I'd never heard, and with conviction from the core of his deteriorating being he shouted at me, 'I'M THE ONE WHO'S DYING—NOT YOU!'

"I continued to stare forward as he ran off to his room. But something began to happen to me. Tears began to fill my eyes and my eyes didn't blink. My body started to tremble uncontrollably. Something inside of me was breaking…or birthing.

"I remember hearing my wife weeping in the kitchen. She saw our son yell at me, and her emotion forced her to the floor. I began to feel her pain—not only of losing her first child and now her 12-year-old son to leukemia…but she'd also lost her husband a long time ago. She felt alone. And it was my fault.

"Still trembling and unable to pull myself together, I stood up, knowing I needed to do something. I walked toward my son's room. I hadn't been in it for months. I opened the door and walked inside. I saw him curled up on the bed. I saw a children's Bible on the floor. I looked around the room and took in the signs of life I'd been missing. I cried out, 'I'm so sorry, son… I'm so sorry. I threw myself on top of him and we wept together. After the initial shock wore off, my son put his arms around my neck. He said, 'Thanks for coming in here daddy.'

My heart broke again. How could I have been so selfish?

"I looked up and saw my wife in the doorway. I could see that she was hopeful, but still hurt. I beckoned for her to come, and she did. The three of us lay in my son's bed together for at least an hour. When we finally got up, we were a family again.

"I didn't waste any more time. I immediately took two weeks off from work and spent every moment with my wife and son. I couldn't get enough. After all, I didn't have much more time with my precious boy. It ended up being about six months. But in that short time, my son taught me more than any other human could. His gratitude for life. His passion for God. His trust that everything would be okay. He lost his fight to cancer, but he taught me how to live. And I've been a changed man ever since.

"I realized that the curse wasn't losing the lives of people I loved. The real curse was that I wasn't really alive, myself. I was dead inside. It was time to choose to live. Now, I choose to live everyday, regardless of the circumstances. It's a matter of perspective. My 12-year-old mentor taught me that. He taught me to believe that God is for me and not against me. And to make the most of the days I'm given."

So you see why Russ made an impression on me!

I've since realized how quick I am to feel sorry for myself. And I've noticed that, when I do, I ignore the pain of others around me. Perhaps worse, I quit seeing the potential in the day—the moment.

We're all dying. But today, we can chose to live.

* * *

Heroes and mentors come in all shapes and sizes. I remember being in my 20's and wishing that I had a particular mentor—perhaps someone wildly successful and important. Then, I looked around me and noticed I already had incredible mentors. There were many people I could learn from—savvy businessmen, hard-working athletes, former military men with great disciplines, avid readers, artist who look at things differently, friends who demonstrated more joy and passion than me, playful kids who reminded me not to take myself so seriously...

There are mentors around you as well. Are you learning from them?

Are you making the most of today?

Experiment

Questions:

Do you know anyone inspiring like Russ? What about Russ's new outlook do you want to embrace for your own life? What attitude is poisoning your experience of today?

Action:

Consider the unexpected, uncelebrated mentors in your life. Call or write one or two of them right now and tell them why they inspire you.

SEEDS OF NEW LIFE

*Very truly I tell you, unless a kernel of wheat falls to the
ground and dies, it remains only a single seed.
But if it dies, it produces many seeds.*
—John 12:24

One of the secrets of the universe is this: Death leads to life.

An acorn on a tree is just an acorn. But if it falls off the tree, dies, and finds it's way to the appropriate soil, it has the capacity to produce more trees. Fruit, vegetables, even animals must die in order to be eaten and to help sustain the lives of other living things.

All go to the same place; all come from dust, and to dust all return.[2] And so we say, from dust to dust. It's the poetic, inevitable, cycle of life.

Ultimately, when a living thing dies, and you put it in the ground, it becomes the ground. It re-enters the creative space of life's design.

Death can produce life. But you have to plant the seeds.

I have experienced this truth in my own life. Death isn't the end. Failure isn't final. Disappointment can lead to dancing. Loss can ultimately produce great gains.

An acorn must fall to the ground before the seed can produce new trees. At first blush, it looks like tragedy. But if you give it time, some scattered seeds from old dead acorns can eventually grow a forest. Death leads to life.

* * *

---

2. *Ecclesiastes 3:20*

Albert Einstein didn't speak until he was four years old. He had teachers that said he would "never amount to much."

Michael Jordan was cut from his high school basketball team. He went home, locked himself in his room and cried.

Walt Disney was fired from a newspaper for "lacking imagination."

The Beatles were rejected by Decca Recording Studios who said, "We don't like their sound—they have no future in show business."

Oprah Winfrey was demoted from her job as news anchor because she "wasn't fit for television."

Arthur Blank and Bernie Marcus were fired from their home improvement jobs. In 1978 they came together to start Home Depot.

These world-changers' legacies live on because *failure is a prerequisite for success.* You wouldn't be who you are without the failure and disappointment you've experienced. The question is, are you leveraging the loss? Are you planting the seeds of death to enable new life spring forth?

Things die. New things are born. Plans fail. New opportunities are born. I am convinced that greater, more purposeful living comes from experiences of death—disappointment, loss, and pain.

* * *

Everyone needs a do-over in some aspect of life.

Have you played with an Etch-a-Sketch? They were the original tablet device, but instead of digital apps, they enabled magnetic art. The two round dials became tools in the hands of great Etch-a-Sketch artists—whom I was not. But the especially helpful feature of the device that made it work for me was the "reset shake." If I messed up my image, there was no eraser. I simply shook the whole tablet in my hand and it was back to blank. Clean slate. Start again.

In golf, they call it a mulligan. In neighborhood street sports, it's a do-over.

For my friend—I'll call her Stacy—the reset was leaving behind a life of stripping.

Stacy didn't intend to be a stripper. A lack of love at home led to unhealthy relationships with boys. Abuse and insecurity left Stacy looking for ways to feel valuable, desirable. One choice led to another and there she was.

"I only started stripping as an experiment—for fun, sort of, and for the money—not because I needed to." But she was still stripping a year later when she hit rock bottom. Feeling lonely, lost, and worthless, she followed her friend to a church event.

"I felt dirty and empty. I told my friend that church was a crutch and that they wouldn't want me there anyway. I guess I only went because I trusted my friend, and I didn't have anywhere else to turn."

It was a 10-week study called Rooted that changed everything for Stacy.

"It was a group of 15 people. They seemed to accept me and not judge me. I even told them my entire story one of the last nights. People cried. They actually cared. They introduced me to real love."

Today, Stacy leads a team of volunteer women who go into strip clubs taking dancers gift bags. The bags have girly items and encouraging notes.

"I just want girls like I was to know that someone cares about them. And if they ever want to change their lives, they have someone they can call—someone who will love them and help them start their life over again."

Do you need a reset?

My friend Dave went back to school at age 50 to learn a new trade. Construction in a down economy wasn't paying the bills. And, at 50-years-old, Dave's back wasn't going to hold up much longer. He enrolled in night classes, while he remodeled homes by day. He studied hard and passed his tests. Dave currently has a new job and is remaking his life.

Do you need a new start?

Jerry is a guy in our church who was addicted to heroin for three years. The average life expectancy of an heroin addict is seven years. Jerry almost died twice from his addiction. After his second overdose and near-death experience, he decided to test recovery. Maybe he could change. I met Jerry for coffee yesterday and he is a new man. He has a job, a girlfriend, and volunteers at church. Jerry has started new addiction meetings in our community and has a long string of days sober.

Jerry, Dave, Stacy, and I, along with millions of others before us, have struggled, failed, gotten stuck and start again. And you can, too.

Here's the thing about resets: they can start anytime, and there are no limits, but if you take them for granted they lose their power. And one day, your time will run out.

Similarly, if you associate a reset with moving to a new city where no one knows you, you might be missing the point. You might just be running.

Resets are not just external, they are internal.

I've had several versions of the iPhone. Anytime I upgrade to the newer model (like an Apple junkie…or sucker) I try to sell the older phone. In order to sell it and not be the victim of identity fraud, I have to clear all my information off the phone. That means a reset to factory settings.

In January, about every-other-year, Hilary and I do the Master Cleanse—drinking nothing but lemon-water and grade B maple syrup for a week. Yeah. The point being to clean out the pipes—flush out the toxins that build up in our systems over time.

Toxins don't just build up in your body. Your mind, heart, and spirit also need regular flushing. We live in a world of mixed messages, destructiveness, hate, selfishness...in general, sin. We need cleansing. And, ultimately, a Reset.

The ancient prophets called for "repenting," which simply means to change your mind, or to turn from one way of living to another.[3] The Apostle Paul pointed to Jesus saying that He makes us "new creations."[4]

In other words, there's a factory reset that can change *everything*. It's like a Divine reclamation and reprogramming. It can happen in a moment[5]...and, it keeps happening everyday.[6]

The reset requires letting-go. I learned, the hard way, that when you obsess about your future, you miss out on life in the present. If you want a new start, you need to let go of old ways that got you to where you are today.

Even if you're discouraged today...even if your past seems to cast a shadow on your future...even though you've tried before and failed...and even if you still think someone else has really screwed up your life...you can have a reset.

Maybe you can't shake your tablet and erase all the consequences, but you can get a new start. You can have renewed hope. You can be remade from the inside out.

Everyday is a new day, full of new opportunity...new possibility...another chance. You just have to receive it.

Death can lead to life. You must simply choose to begin again.

"Though no one can go back and make a brand new start, anyone can start from now and make a brand new ending."
—Carl Bard

Experiment

Question:
How have you seen death turn into new life—or become a new start? In what ways do you need a fresh start today?

Action:
Put a sign or note beside your bed that says: *Welcome to a brand new day! Anything can happen.*

---

3.   *Matthew 3:2*

4.   *2 Cor 5:17*

5.   *Acts 16:31*

6.   *2 Cor 4:16*

Consider beginning again by praying a simple prayer. I know this might seem weird, but it also just might open the door to a new beginning...

God, on my own, I tend to make a mess of my life. I need a reset—and new start. I want to learn what it means to live how You designed me to live. I want to be a new creation. Help me to begin again...with You.

PRESS BOX FUNERAL

"Death is inevitable. And something will have to be done with your body." —Funeral Director, interview

Death is big business. Over two and half million Americans die in the U.S. every year. And that number is expected to go up 30% as the Baby Boomer generation ages. Americans already spend $17 billion dollars a year on death services—their final expense.

Here are some more fascinating stats about the industry of death:

- The death rate spikes in the cold and flu season—December through February are the months when the most people die.
- Caskets have model names, like cars, to attract different levels of consumers.
- There are 1.5 million caskets sold every year—75% are metal, 25% are wooden.
- In the Philippines, many caskets are hung on mountain faces and over cliffs, so the deceased are "closer" to heaven.
- Average cost of a burial is $6,500; cremation average is $1,600 and a growing trend.
- A crematorium incinerates at 1,600 degrees. Artificial hips, knees, etc. don't burn, but are recycled.
- Fans are still leaving baseballs, gloves, hotdogs, and beer at Babe Ruth's grave.
- There are companies that, literally, make diamonds from ashes.
- A man once bid $4.6 million for a crypt above Marilyn Monroe.
- Obesity in the U.S. has changed the sizing of caskets. Many now can hold people up to 600 pounds.
- Prices in a cemetery are set like real estate anywhere—location, location, location.

When I was a kid, my dad once joked with me, "You see that fancy field over there? That's a very expensive cemetery. People are just dying to get in there."

Why do we spend so much money and exert so much effort honoring and caring for the remains of the deceased. They're dead, after all. What do they care? What did you do with your pet hamster when it died? Your dog? Cat? You probably cried, reflected, and buried them. Without an honoring response to death, a life seems less special.

We mourn, reflect upon, and honor the dead because we feel we must—and we believe that somehow it matters.

There is something in us—in all of us—that senses an invisible truth: What we do in this life matters in the next.

* * *

Chad was the student chosen (out of a school of 2,200 students) to be the life claimed by a pretend car accident at his high school assembly. You know the kind? Where the car is mangled in the center of campus and a pretend emergency scene hopes to scare kids into thinking about the importance of sober, text-free driving?

The program is not new. But for Chad, and his dad, it was haunting.

Here's an email I got from Chuck, Chad's dad:

The Accident

Today started like most days, but today was different because I knew I was going to watch my 18 year old son be pronounced dead at the scene of a car accident.

When we got to the football stadium at the high school we were taken to the press box so no students would see us. My younger son, four nieces and nephews (who attend the same school), and two of my sisters were brought into the press box with my wife and I. We sat and watched as the 2,200 students filed into the stadium completely unaware of what was about to take place. When everyone was seated the drama began to unfold. There were two big tarps down on the field, each covering the cars that had been set to demonstrate a horrific accident. My son and the three other seniors involved were already in the cars under the tarps. Suddenly the tarps were pulled off and the horrific scene was right there in front of everyone. I have to admit that even though I knew what was coming I was overcome with emotion when I saw my son trapped and motionless under the car he was in. A police radio came over the loud speakers telling of an accident at NGHS. Sirens started to sound in the distance. It took 3 minutes for the ambulance, fire trucks, and police cars to get to the scene of the accident. The crowd of 2,200 kids sat very quietly as the teams approached. I could only stare at the mangled car that imprisoned my son.

After using the Jaws of Life to free another student, they got to my son. I heard the words over the radio, "passenger deceased." I had tried to prepare myself for this all week but when I heard those words it tore me up inside. My wife was sobbing and the aunts, brother, and cousins all sat in a state of shock. The firemen walked away obviously disappointed at seeing a young person lifeless in the car. They left my son in the car while they brought the driver of the second car back in front of the crowd. They began to test him for DUI and it was obvious that he was under age and way over the limit. We all watched as they placed handcuffs on him and took him away in the police car.

Next they came and pulled my son from the car and placed him in a body bag. It is hard to watch your son look so lifeless and go through this. He was taken away to complete silence in the stadium. Then the principal walked out on to the field with his phone in his hand and acted out the call he was making—to us!

"Mr. and Mrs. Scott, on behalf of NGHS I want to share with you how sorry we are for your loss. We are all heart broken here at the school. Chad was such a wonderful young man. He was a great student and exceptional athlete. We will greatly miss his leadership. We want you to know that our hearts are broken for you and your family." This is the part I was not prepared for. I had played out the accident scenario, and even though seeing it was hard I was making it through. But this phone call hit us all like a ton of bricks. Everyone was in tears in the press box. There were a lot of tears in the crowd. This is the call no parent ever wants to receive.

The Service

*Two days later, the school held a mock-funeral for Chad. All 2,200 students filed into the stadium as soft music played over the PA system. On the field was a casket with Chad's football jersey and pictures. We (the family and speakers) walked down the track in front of the whole assembly. As we approached the Casket and saw the pictures of Chad I had to remind myself over and over that we are just pretending. The family all sat down in the seats in front of the Casket and then Pastor Sharrett got up and delivered his message. It was powerful. He reflected on James 4:14: **Yet you do not***

know what your life will be like tomorrow. You are just a vapor that
appears for a little while and then vanishes away. He challenged the
students to make an impact with their lives. He shared about the amazing
legacy Chad had "left" in his short time here on earth. He said, "Choices
we make today will decide our future tomorrow."

The message was powerful and the kids were challenged. They were challenged to make good decisions while driving a car but more importantly
they were challenged to think about **life**.

Take your seat at the top of the stadium. Your Near Death Experience is well
underway.

Imagine seeing this scene play out from a seat in the press box. You see the
mangled car. This accident is horrible—how could anyone survive? You look
closer and notice a lifeless body pressed against the steering wheel of the car…it's
yours. You family is in shock, your mother is weeping. Your father tries to hold
in his tears—trying to be strong for the family—but when He gets the call…
he breaks…

Experiment

Questions:

What do people place on or next to your casket? Jerseys, artwork, flags, banners,
balance sheets…? What are you known for? And who are in the pictures that
decorate your memorial? Who sits on stage? What do they miss about you? How
will their lives be better because of yours? When the speakers get up to share,
what will they say? You may not have accomplished all you had hoped, but have
you lived in a manner in which you can be proud?

It's okay if your answer to this point is, "no." But it's not okay if you do
nothing about it.

Actions:

Go to a funeral. Call a local church and ask what funerals are scheduled for that
week. Go, sit in the back, and listen…and think…and feel.

How do you know what your life will be like tomorrow? Your
life is like the morning fog—it's here a little while, then it's gone.
                              —James 4:14 (NLT)

Of Grave Importance

Things that Matter

ORDERING AFAIRS

*"You have brains in your head and feet in your shoes
You can steer yourself any direction you choose.
You're on your own and you know what you know
And you are the one who'll decide where to go."*
—Dr. Suess

LAST DANCE

"When you dance, your purpose is not to get to a certain place on the floor. It's to enjoy each step along the way."
—Wayne Dyer

Dr. James Wolf is losing his battle with pancreatic cancer. His 25-year-old daughter, Rachel, is devastated that she only has a few more months with her dad. He's her doctor. He's her dad. He's her hero.

Like most little girls, Rachel grew up dreaming of the day when she would dress up in a white dress, walk down an aisle with her father, marry the man of her dreams, and have a daddy-daughter dance before riding into the sunset with her new husband. But with no wedding on the horizon, it's clear that Dr. Wolf won't live to see her daughter get married.

Unwilling to accept that her father wouldn't be at her wedding, Rachel made a way.

She designed an invitation—just one. It was to her father. And it was invitation to their wedding day dance.

Rachel's plan was to have a wedding event just to dance with her father before he was unable to walk. She figured she needed to pull it off in about two weeks.

The word got around quickly in their town near Sacramento, California. The local news station picked up the story, and in a matter of hours the entire event was booked and paid for. All kinds of local businesses donated their time and equipment—including a tux, wedding dress, DJ, and limousine. Ten days later, Rachel danced with her father to "Cinderella" by Steven Curtis Chapman.

"I want to tell dads who have little girls, videotape you and your daughter dancing, but save it. You never know what's going to happen," she said.

Rachel doesn't plan to watch the video of her dancing with her father until her actual wedding day. On that day, the video will play, and she her dad will dance—if only on screen.

* * *

I had my annual physical shortly after turning 25-years-old. My doctor playfully broke the news to me: "You're dying."

"Ha," I muttered.

"Well… I'm kind of serious," he said. "At approximately 25-years-old humans stop growing. And you know what that means? We start the process of dying."

Dr. Downer.

Yet it's a reality you'd do well to remember. We have a terminal condition. We're all dying…it's just a matter of when.

* * *

May the Lord bless his people with peace
and happiness and let them celebrate.
—Psalm 64:10

There are many holidays, birthdays, weddings, parties, and special occasions, and yet we still don't celebrate enough. What if you looked for the ways that God blesses you and made a big deal about them? What if you became the kind of person who appreciated life as you know it? What if you celebrated others at every opportunity?

I'm not a big dancer, but I probably should be. We dance because life is worth celebrating. We dance to live in the moment. We dance because we're still alive.

Dance. Throw a party. Spend time with the people you love.

Experiment

Question:

Who are the more important people in your life? Do they know it? Do they know how special they are to you? What would you do if you only had another month with someone you most loved?

Action:

Schedule a "last dance." It doesn't have to be an actual dance—it can be anything: a date, a party, a game, a song, a walk… But do something special with the people who matter most to you. And tell them why they are so special.

THE MAIN THING

"The key to the ability to change is a changeless sense of who
you are, what you are about and what you value."
—Stephen R. Covey

There is an Italian restaurant Newport Beach called Mama D's. It's famous in Orange Country. The first time I went, I was impressed. The server was attentive and kind. The atmosphere was fun and inviting. And, most importantly, the food was great.

The second time I went to Mama D's I was taking food to-go. Hilary called it in and I was picking it up. I parked in the small parking lot behind the restaurant, and went in the back door. I was immediately greeted by a guy in tie—I assumed him to be the manager.

"Welcome to Mama D's," He said.

"Thanks," I responded.

"You here for a pick-up order?"

"I am."

"Great, we'd love to help you that. Here is the pick-up counter; someone will be right with you."

He wasn't kidding. By the time I looked up, two people were coming toward me. The first gave me a plate of fresh-baked bread, a dish with special olive oil for dipping, and a glass of ice water. The person right behind him got my name, grabbed my order, and took my credit card. When I signed the receipt, the guy walked around the counter with my to-go boxes, and asked me where I parked.

"I'll walk these to your car," he offered.

"Uh, ok." I was caught off guard, but I just went with it.

When we got to my car, he safely placed the food in the back seat and then extended his hand. "Have a great night Mr. Anderson." He wasn't looking for a tip, because before I had time to respond, he was skipping back inside to pass along more mind-blowing service to other customers.

My experience at Mama D's impressed me so much, I told everyone I talked to about their incredible service for the next two days. On my next visit, I noticed the Mama D's guiding vision statement with their values at the bottom. I took a picture so you could see it here

❧Our Vision❧

We at Mama D's are Proud to be the

"WORLD CLASS CRAZY ONES"

On our watch, we want to do something
extraordinary with our gifts and talents.
History will be the judge, but the script is
ours. We are on an adventure to blow the
doors off "business as usual." We are here to
make a difference in the world, and a world of
difference. We are extremely committed and
passionate about a culture built on loyal
relationships, within our team and the world,
that are generated by Genuine Care, Fun,

Heart, Honor, and Happiness,

❧ONE PERSON AT A TIME❧

When your vision and values are clear, decisions are easy.

I was a business major in college and I've started and led several organizations. One of the first and foundational questions of any start-up endeavor is, "What are we here to do?" In other words, "What's our *main thing?* How are we different than others? What makes us unique? Why do we do what we do?"

Every good organization gets very clear about what they do, and what they don't do. There are an infinite number of ways to contribute to society. But a business must start out by choosing one. Do one thing well, and you just might be able to contribute more.

Similarly, you should be clear about a project you undertake. For example, the Mission Statement for this book could be: *To inspire personal reflection, renewed perspective, and passion for life by leveraging the reality of death.*

Then, the idea would be to let this statement guide the writing process. Research or experience that was interesting to me but outside of this focus would be left out of the book.

Values, then, whether for a person, project, or company, should add further context to the defining mission statement. My values as I've written this book have been:

- **creativity** (I value intrigue and a "hook"),
- **clarity** (I want the concepts to be simple and understandable), and
- **action** (I want to promote immediate next steps)

Consider your own set of personal values... What rank as the highest four values for your life? Here is a list to get your started:

- faith
- health
- fitness
- learning
- work
- play
- friendships
- family
- fun
- adventure
- art
- creativity
- science
- progress
- problem-solving
- money
- nature
- service

Here are some questions to help:

- What are you most passionate about?
- What have people affirmed in you that they most appreciate?
- Where do you see yourself in ten years?
- When do you feel most alive?
- How can you state your main thing (mission/vision) is a succinct sentence?

I wrote a mission statement for my life when I was 25 years old. After going through a divorce, failing in two start-up businesses, and losing two homes I thought I must have been wrong about my mission. If not wrong, then I blew it. I ruined it.

But, in reality, I was right all along. I had just been going about it in the wrong way.

I revised my life mission statement slightly—mainly to get the focus off myself and onto others. But the essence is the same: *To honor God with my life by encouraging, equipping, and empowering others to be all that they were designed to be.* That statement is specific enough to focus me, but also leaves some room for different expressions based on things I value:

- I love and build into my family first and foremost
- I care for and lead people at Mariners Church in Huntington Beach
- I write books and speak to crowds
- I coach leaders

But all of these things center around encouraging, equipping, and empowering others (to be who they were designed to be).

Since I was young, my dad observed in me that I was a leader and an encourager. That's been reaffirmed though-out my life. Yet when I've compared myself to the greatest leaders and communicators I've known, it's caused me to get insecure and discouraged. "I'm not like them... I'm not as influential... I'm not as brilliant." But that's stupid. And it's a trap you and I can't afford fall into.

- I'm just getting started.
- God designed me differently.

Comparison can paralyze you from making progress. The key is to be the best possible version of you. Understand how God's made you. Enjoy how God's made you. And develop the strengths He's given you.

Here are a few other notable mission statements to spark your imagination:

- **Walt Disney:** My mission in life is to make people happy.
- **Apple** is committed to bringing the best personal computing experience to students, educators, creative professionals, and consumers around the world through its innovative hardware, software, and internet offerings.
- **Zappos:** To provide the best customer service possible.
- **Rebecca, Rancher:** My life's mission is to protect and save early American farm animals such at the American Guinea hog and the Ben Franklin turkey from extinction.
- **Bob, Business Manager:** I want to continuously foster and promote cooperation in every environment I find myself—helping people and organizations come together for the greater good.
- **Tracy, Personal Trainer:** I will help people reach their potential in health and fitness—learning to love themselves while making the most of their bodies.

This could be a significant turning point for you. Today could set, change, or confirm the course of your life. This could be the day that your grandchildren talk about as the day your legacy changed. This could be the spark that sets new events into motion. Today might be the day that you risk the comfort of the life you know for the hope of the life that could be. Maybe, just maybe, you'll allow the whispers in your soul to turn into commitments in your day. Or, I guess you could just float through life aimlessly.

Mission Statement: In a sentence, the main thing you aim to contribute with your life.
Values: Beliefs, ideals, or priorities of highest significance to your life.

"How many of us have become drunks and drug addicts...
succumbed to painkillers, gossip, and compulsive cell-phone
use, simply because we don't do that thing that our hearts...
are calling us to?"
—Steven Pressfield, The War of Art

Experiment

Question:
What are the few things you value most that inform how you live your life?

Action:
Write your Personal Mission Statement. Ask yourself, "What is my calling, my life's aim? What inspires me most?" Put it in a journal and on an index card. Keep the card with you or posted somewhere you'll see it regularly.

"One thing I do: Forgetting what is behind and straining
toward what is ahead, I press on toward the goal to win
the prize for which God has called me..."
—Philippians 3:13-14

FOCUS

"Where focus goes, energy flows."
—Tony Robbins

The legendary Rocky Marciano is famous for being the only Heavyweight Champion boxer to retire undefeated. At only 190 pounds, few expected much from Rocky in his early years as a boxer. Rocky began boxing in the Army, mostly as a way to avoid kitchen duties. He showed some promise, but his true desire was to be a professional baseball player. In 1947, after his discharge from the Army, Rocky earned a try-out with the Chicago Cubs as a catcher, but was soon released because of his inability to accurately throw from home plate to second base. The following year, he turned professional in the boxing ring.

In her book, "On Boxing," Joyce Carol Oates studies Rocky Marciano and the unique level of focus and preparation rituals that cause him such unparalleled success.

"Marciano was willing to exclude himself from the world, including his wife and family, for as long as three months before a fight. Apart from the grueling physical ordeal of this period and the obsessive reoccupation with diet and weight and muscle tone, Marciano concentrated on one thing: the upcoming fight. Every minute of his life was defined in terms of the opening second of the fight. In his training camp the opponent's name was never mentioned in Marciano's hearing, nor was boxing as a subject discussed. In the final month Marciano would not write a letter since a letter related to the outside world. During the last ten days before a fight he would see no mail, take no telephone calls, meet no new acquaintances. During the week before the fight he would not shake hands. Or go for a ride in a car, however brief. No new foods! No dreaming of the morning after the fight! For all that was not the fight had to be excluded from consciousness. When Marciano worked out with a punching bag he saw his opponent before him, when he jogged he saw his opponent close beside him, no doubt when he slept he 'saw' his opponent constantly—as the cloistered monk or nun chooses by an act of fanatical will to 'see' only God."

Rocky Marciano was a man of laser focus. His level of focus was certainly extreme. Even if your methods of focus look different, focus is your friend.

When you were a kid, did you ever use a magnifying glass and sunlight to fry a small bug? (That's terrible. What's wrong with you?) I've heard that the magnifying glass catches the sunlight and intensifies it, focusing a direct, high-powered beam of hot light onto the bug, shortening his already meager lifespan. In other words, it creates a very small laser. Focused light can be so powerful that it can cut through metal.

What do you think you would be capable of if you got laser-focused? I mean, instead of all the television, social media, and distracting time-suckers... What if you got really focused? What if you got really clear about your Main Thing, or your top priorities? What could you do?

Part of staying focused is being willing to kill good things. Jim Collins has said, "Good is the enemy of Great."[1] To get laser-focused on the Main Things, you will have to kill a lot of other things. Even other nice, warm, fuzzy things if they are distracting you from the ultimate things.

> *"The secret to concentration is elimination."*
> —Dr Howard Heinrichs

---

1. *Good To Great, Jim Collins*

Every time you say "yes" to something, you're saying "no" to something else. This is how men end up on their deathbeds wishing they hadn't said "no" to their kids and wives as much as they did…Wishing they could go back and reprioritize their lives—and keep the main thing the main thing.

When Hilary and I were asked to take over Mariners Church in Huntington Beach the first decision we made was to move into the center of town. That way, we were surrounding ourselves with the realities of the community. But the reality of moving into the center of Huntington was that we would have to down-size. Huntington is expensive, and we'd have to squeeze our lives into a small condo. But the upside of down-sizing is that it forced us to simplify our lives. With less stuff there are fewer distractions.

In addition, I turned down various other opportunities, trips, and engagements so that I could focus on bringing the energy and passion that was needed to create new momentum for the church. It's just been one year, but it's working.

Do you "less is more?" Because many things distract you from the few things that really matter. You've begun to get clear about the things that really matter in your life. Now practice saying "no" to the stuff that matters less.

Experiment

Question:
What are the things that distract you from focusing on your top priorities?

Action:
Create a t-chart. If you are going to be a more focused person, you're going to have to kill some distractions.

Focus on		Kill

FLAME

Pumbaa: *Hey, Timon, ever wonder what those sparkly dots are up there?*
Timon: *Pumbaa, I don't wonder; I know.*
Pumbaa: *Oh. What are they?*
Timon: *They're fireflies. Fireflies that, uh... got stuck up on that big bluish-black thing.*
Pumbaa: *Oh, gee. I always thought they were balls of gas burning billions of miles away.*
Timon: *Pumbaa, with you, everything's gas.*
– The Lion King

Stars are massive balls of fire. And these great balls of fire have guided journeyers through the dark for thousands of years. Humans, birds, seals, and even dung beetles use the stars to navigate their way at night.

Everyone has their guiding flames. The question is, where are they leading you?

* * *

I'm not a pyromaniac, but I'm fascinated by fire. Our solar system revolves around a sun—a ball of fire. There are billions of stars, like the sun, in galaxies far, far away that also burn. Our sun is so hot that if our earth were any closer, it would fry every living thing.

More than burning, fire gives light. If you're in the dark, you light a match so that you can see. Fire also warms us and cooks our food. Many great conversations have happened around a fire. Fire can be used as a signal to get our attention.

In the bible, fire is used in many interesting ways. Here are a few:

- God appeared to Moses in a bush that was on fire.[2]
- God led the Israelites through the desert with a pillar of fire.[3]
- God came down on Mt. Sinai in fire.[4]
- God sent fire to engulf a soaking wet altar.[5]
- God's Spirit came down on the disciples in tongues of fire.[6]

---

2. *Exodus 3*   3. *Exodus*   4. *Exodus 19*   5. *I Kings 18*   6. *Acts 2*

There are many other instances where God used fire to make a point. Throughout the Old Testament, God uses fire as a sign, a guide, or a demonstration. But in the final instance (Acts 2), God sends His Holy Spirit as fire. The Spirit—signified as fire—is believed to reside in everyone who invites God to lead his or her life. So, the life of Jesus is no longer confined to one human body, but is being worked out in billions of souls around the world.

So, when people have said, "someone lit a fire in that kid," they are actually (unknowingly) referencing this mysterious reality that God's Spirit ignites, inspires, and leads people to live more full and meaningful lives. When people say, "Jesus lives in my heart", that's a cute way of explaining the reality that we are referring to here—that His invisible Spirit is in them—whispering, prompting, comforting, encouraging.

Therefore, if you feel like you're lacking that fire, you simply need to ask, and invite your Creator to restore the relationship He's always intended for you, and then fuel your life from the inside out.

Then, follow the fire.

There's a prompting, a leading inside of you that's telling you something. There's fire that's fueling your passion. You're passionate about certain things for a reason. There are injustices that compel you to action. There are moments that prompt tears of joy or empathy. There are images that speak to your soul. There are activities that make you feel alive.

In 1981, *Chariots of Fire* was nominated for seven Academy Awards and won four, including Best Picture. The film got its title from a line in a William Blake poem, "bring me my chariot of fire."

In the movie, Eric Liddell is born to missionary parents serving in China. He, too, feels called to serve as a missionary in China, but first he is drawn to competitive running. Questioned about his priorities by his devout Christian sister, Liddell responds, "When I run, I feel God's pleasure."

There will be something that you do, that when you do it, you feel God's pleasure. It might be your vocation, it might be a hobby, it might something else altogether. But whatever it is, follow it. That's your chariot of fire.

What if you currently have nothing you're passionate about? Choose something. Choose something meaningful, in alignment with the priorities we're discussing in this book, and choose to be passionate.

Feelings follow action. I don't enjoy the idea of working out when I'm at home in my underwear. But when I force myself to go and run or lift and sweat, I always feel better after. The more I remember the positive feelings, the more likely I am to become passionate about exercise.

Similarly, you can become passionate about the changes you want to see in your life. The thought of change might terrify or frustrate you today, but if you take the time to learn truths, refocus your mind, take simple action steps (all the ingredients of this book), you will soon find yourself passionately inspired.

* * *

Side note...

Addiction is misdirected passion. When you're disappointed by something in your life (even subconsciously), you seek a thrill/excitement elsewhere. That pattern becomes an addiction. And addictions suck your passion from the appropriate places in your life and supercharge other areas with dangerous obsession.

If you're struggling to find passion in your life, it's probably stuck in the service of an immediate gratification pattern. My advice: Don't just try to white-knuckle and stop the bad behavior. Redirect your energy and replace the addiction with a healthy passion. If you want to go north, you can't get there by facing south. You have to turn around and go in a new direction.

* * *

There is a race for you to run. There is a ball of gas that will light your path. And God wants to fan a flame inside of you to see to see you through.

Experiment

Question:

What are the guiding influences of your life? And what is a passion that inspires you? (If you don't yet sense a passion, what is a passion that'd you want?)

Action:

Write a letter to your children (or future children) about the things in life you're most passionate. Inspire them to live the kind of lives you hope they will live.

AWARE

"The traveler sees what he sees.
The tourist sees what he has come to see."
—G.K. Chesterton

When I was a kid, my dad worked with an organization called Young Life, and the people involved had a profound impact on me. In fact, it was the people that mattered to my dad. He has told me that anytime his attention shifted from loving people to some lesser thing, he missed the point. One night "the point" got all of our attention.

It was the end of the year. The group of about 80 high school students were meeting in the backyard of a home—a home owned by someone who understood the value of giving teenagers a safe place to be themselves. It was the last time this group would be together. About 30 of them would be graduating the following week and moving on to the next season of life. It was a special night—a send-off.

Dad was there because he provided leadership and oversight for a bunch of groups like that one. He visited different groups on different nights and weeks. That night, he took me with him. We sat in the back and I tried to act like a grown-up.

There was a woman who helped coordinate, and clearly the students liked her. She spent time every week on the high school campus, tutoring students, going to their sporting events, talking to girls about their boy trouble... really, just being a friend of students. And that night, what the students didn't know—and what my dad didn't know—was that she prepared a song she wrote just for them.

Now pause here for a moment. Public speaking is the number one fear of most humans. I speak in public multiple times per week and yet I still get nervous. Palms sweat, the mind threatens to go blank, people in the crowd look unhappy... You know what mean? Are your palms sweating just thinking about it?

So this 40-something woman cared so much about these kids that she wrote them a song. Then, she learned the three most basic guitar chords, and she practiced like crazy in order to play and sing the song for this special night—the "going away" night for many of these students.

The time had come. Energy was high. Girls were sitting on boyfriends' laps. Boyfriends were punching the guy the next to them in an effort to still seem tough. Lots of these kids had too much metal in their face to pass airport security. But as a ten-year-old, these were coolest kids I'd ever seen.

One of the other adults shared for just a few moments from the bible. He told a story about Jesus but I don't remember which one. He gave the students advice about how to have a great summer and how to stay connected to God and to people who will encourage them and love them. Then he introduced the woman.

I could tell that my dad was nervous. It seemed like the meeting was over.

The high school students with chains and tattoos seemed like they had reached their capacity for paying attention. I, too, was ready to go. So when the woman walked up and nervously sat down on a stool with a guitar, my dad shifted his weight and had a concerned look on his face.

"Well, most of you know me," she started. "But you probably didn't know that I play the guitar. That's because I don't." Light laughter. "I just had someone teach me a couple chords so I could sing a song I wrote for all of you. I'm a little nervous, so bear with me." Never a good disclaimer.

She hit the first note but it wasn't right. She shifted her fingers and started again. It was clunky. Even at ten, I knew this was bad. I was sweating on her behalf.

Her song lyrics were on a piece of paper that she taped to the top of her guitar. She looked at the paper, looked up in an attempt to make eye contact with a graduating student, then looked back at the paper. My dad looked around, anxiously assessing the situation.

Later, I heard my dad talk about this event on numerous occasions.

"I almost panicked," he recounted. "I thought she was dead. I thought these kids would turn on her. I mean, kids can be cruel and insensitive. And she was not good. She was trying, it was a loving gesture, but I stood up in the back thinking I might need to dive in front and protect her from flying objects. I'd certainly have to try and transition this to a better close."

The crowd was silent. My dad was fidgety. My sympathy-sweat increased. And the woman…she was beating on the guitar, pitch all over the place, desperately trying to convey the words from her heart to her students.

It was a tense couple minutes. Then it ended. She hit the final chord and nervously looked up. My dad braced himself for the worst. He feared for the woman. Such a sweet woman.

And then, it happened. The crowd erupted in cheers and applause!

Clapping…hollers…shouts…even a standing ovation.

From what I could tell, it was all the graduating seniors who rushed the stage area. They hugged her. A few were crying. Our tone-deaf-woman-with-a-huge-heart was crying and smiling ear to ear. It was pandemonium, alright. But the good kind.

I looked at my dad. He had a tear in his eye. He put his hand on my shoulder and shook his head. We couldn't believe what we were seeing.

Later, my dad said something that has stuck with me all these years:

"I almost missed it. I was so concerned with her performance, and with how she would be received. I almost missed a miracle that night."

As I've grown up from that ten-year-old boy, I fear how many times I've missed the point, or miracle, or significance in a situation. I'm certain there have been many days that I've been so concerned with my performance and with public approval that I've missed the heart of the matter. I've missed the beauty of the moment. I've missed the invisible work of God in the lives of people. When you sweat the small, superficial stuff, you miss the stuff of significance.

What is it that you pay attention to? What might you be missing?

Experiment

Question:
When was the last time you simply sat, observed, and appreciated life happening around you? What do you obsess about that distracts you from the beauty of the moment?

Action:
Go to a park. Sit on a bench. Wear something that doesn't make you look like a creeper. Watch people. Notice what they're doing…how they're doing it… what seems to matter to them…why do you believe they're at the park. Then go further: What does their demeanor tell you about their day, their life? Notice. Then notice more.

In doing so, you begin to train yourself to be more aware. There's a person beyond their performance. There's a story below the surface.

"Tell me to what you pay attention and I will tell you who you are."
—Jose Ortega

LOOK AND SEE

"Get used to disappointment."
—The Man in Black, The Princess Bride

Think about the last time you were in the market for a new car. When you began to narrow down your selection to one or two different vehicles, something interesting likely began to happen. You started noticing your favorite cars everywhere you looked. The car would fly by you on freeway; it'd be in the parking spot next to you; it'd be on television. All of the sudden it seemed like the car you wanted was everywhere.

The car is not everywhere. Your brain is biased. You told you brain what you love; now your brain is showing it to you. Your eyes will see what you mind has already locked in on.

I'd like to call it the Phenomenon of Subconscious Noticing.

Phenomenon of Subconscious Noticing: The subconscious mind locks onto an idea or a material thing and signals your conscious mind whenever an observation or a connection can be made. The car might have always been there. But once your mind locks in the car's prioritized position, you notice it.

This reality could change your life for the better—immediately:

If you train your mind to look for the good—in people, places, and opportunities—that's what you'll see. Just like if you train your mind to look for disappointment, you will find it.

I know of a man who had become a hermit in his old age. He worked as a teacher and then administrator in an inner city school in Los Angeles. During his tenure there, the school (at least in his view) went downhill. Test scores dropped while instances of bad behavior seemed to skyrocket. Over time, the aging man grew to hate his job. Worse, he began to hate teenagers. When he could take it no longer, he retired and moved to a small town in Oklahoma. There, he barely made time for his own grandkids, let alone any other young people. In fact, he quickly earned the reputation in the neighborhood of "the grumpy old man."

One year, on Thanksgiving, a bold 16-year-old girl with a compassionate heart decided to check-in on the old man. After all, she justified, it was Thanksgiving, and there were no cars parked in front of the old man's house. Even though her family tried talking her out of it, saying things like, "You know this can't go well," and, "Honey, you're sweet, but this man doesn't care about sweet." But she was determined. She knew the old man was lonely, and it didn't matter to her if he was mean, harsh, and rude. She was wanted to test out the impact her kindness could make.

So she took a pie over. (This, too, frustrated the family a little, as she took one of the two delicious pumpkin pies saying, "But we have two!") She walked right past the lawn gnome holding a sign, "Retired: Do Not Disturb!" She approached the door, confident of her good intentions. She pressed the doorbell but couldn't determine if worked or not. So she followed up with a firm knock. Nothing. She knocked again. This time she heard some stirring inside. He was coming.

The heavy door creaked and opened slowly; his furrowed face peered around its edge and he looked down at the sweet 16-year-old with obvious irritation in his eyes. "What do you want?"

"Happy Thanksgiving. I just wanted to tell you that and to offer you some pie." Pause. No response… So she continued, "Do you have any friends or family with you today?"

"Nope. But you can tell *your* family that this is how I like it. And I don't like pie." He gestured behind her. She turned and saw her family quickly closing the curtains to hide their curious stares.

"Sorry about that," she said. "This was only my idea. I just wanted you to know that people cared."

"Well, I'm not sure I believe you. See you at Christmas," he said sarcastically as he closed the door.

Pie still in-hand, and undaunted by the old man's grumpiness, she made a mental note: See you at Christmas.

Christmas morning she was back on the doorstep; this time with cookies. Several strong knocks produced no response. She peered her head in the side window and saw the television on. "He's gotta be in there," she thought. She walked along the side of the house and into the backyard. Still no sounds. As she approached the backdoor, she saw that it was open. In fact, looking at the frame, it appeared the door had been forced open. "Maybe this is a bad idea," she thought. But she continued with the same courage that brought her over in the first place.

"Sir," she hollered as she began into the back of the house. She thought she heard something and followed the noise. "Are you alright?"

She opened what would be his bedroom door and saw the old man bound with duct tape on the floor next to his bed. She cried out and moved toward him. She set him free and then called 911. It turned out that the little girl wasn't the only person who had noticed that this retired old man was continually alone without visitors. He had been robbed two nights earlier. His two assailants bound him and took various items of value. The old man had attempted to get himself to safety but broke his collarbone rolling off the bed. It was too painful to roll or move anymore. He just waited—knowing that the likelihood of help arriving was slim.

In the 30+ hours the old man was a prisoner his own home, he reflected on his life. He prayed, begged for mercy, regretted isolating decisions, and was desperate for a second chance. Then came his 16-year-old angel of compassion.

If you met the man today, you'd discover a very different old man. His outlook reverted back to the young man who went into teaching in Los Angeles in his twenties: with the hope of making a difference. He has a childlike glimmer in his eye. He's done his best to reconcile relationships. He appreciates his life and the lives of others. He's a different man, and he credits his "awakening" to a 16-year-old girl that cared enough to knock.

Let's turn this on ourselves. Where has your outlook gone sour? How have you allowed discouragement, disillusionment, or difficulty cause you to look at your life or at others through negative lenses?

Regardless of your justifications, you're cheating your experience of life. You're focusing on the wrong things, and it's going to make you into a person you don't want to be.

Optimism: Trusting that God is good, and good is on the way.

Optimistic Outlook: Looking for the good in every situation.

If you look for the good around you, you'll find it. If you look for the good in others, you'll discover some. If you expect negative circumstances to produce positive results, you'll learn from everything. If you choose to be joyful and content, despite the situation, you'll live a life that inspires others.

Everyone has an outlook on life—an expectation for how the world should work. Some have call it their "blueprint" for life. Their blueprint tells them how life should be. Two plus two should equal four. If I put in this effort, then this should happen. In marriage, this should be what I experiences. In my finances, I should achieve the quality of life I want by a certain age. When it comes to health, here's what I expect...

Your blueprint sets your expectations. You might not realize you have expectations until you get into the situation—the marriage, the new job, etc. But you'll certainly realize it when your expectations aren't met.

When expectations match experience, you're happy. But when your expectations do not match your experience, you're disappointed.

Disappointment: Unmet expectations.

Thus,

Expectations = Experience » happy

Expectations ≠ Experience » unhappy

If you find yourself your unhappy, disappointed, discontent with part or the whole of your life, something needs to change. You might think it's just life... "I need to get used to disappointment...I don't deserve the things I want... God doesn't care about my needs...etc." But that's crap. You're going to end up making yourself miserable. You'll end up a grumpy person who isolates yourself.

Instead, change something. Here are your options:

1.   You can change your experience...or,

2.   You can change your expectation.

And here's how you determine which thing to choose: If you can change your experience without compromise your Main Thing or guiding values, then, by all means, change your experience. Move into the new house. Get a different job. Start your own business. Break-up with your boyfriend. Go to the gym five times a week. Make the changes in your day-to-day experience of life that you can make—change the things you can…the things that lead to a more full experience of life. Change them!

And yet there will some things that cannot change. Some things that are out of your control. Or some changes that would be too costly to your character or your family. Things like divorce, or the death of a loved one, or the loss of physical capacity due to injury, etc. In these instances—with regard to experiences and circumstances that you cannot change—you, instead, must choose to change your *expectations*.

If your spouse hasn't lived up to your hopes and expectations, change your expectations. Embrace who they are and build them up with no strings attached. You might feel like it's a lack of integrity but you're wrong. It's killing your pride, and it will give life to your spouse.

If your financial or career trajectory hasn't lived up to your expectations, and if now is not the time to pursue something new, change your outlook. Enjoy what you have. Appreciate the people you work with. Find the good in the situation. You don't *need* more. You might want more, but if you can't enjoy and appreciate what you have today, you won't be able to enjoy or appreciate what you'll gain in the future.

I asked three friends of mine who is "rich" in their eyes. My friend just out of collage making $25,000 this year said that "rich" to him was his friend who landed a good corporate job making $50,000. I asked someone in their late 20's making $50,000 this year who is "rich" to them. She said that her girlfriend cutting hair at a salon in Newport Beach is rich because she has few obligations and will make over $100,000 this year. I asked that young hair-stylist in Newport Beach who is rich and she pointed to the guy who owned the salon saying, "between his three salons he easily makes a quarter million, and he'll probably open more."

And my guess is that if I asked the salon owner "who is rich in your eyes," he would not have identified himself, but some friend of his who is at least twice as wealthy as him. And such is the outlook of most human beings.

The sad thing is, most people have an expectation that they will be happy when they arrive at some future place or status. When I get married, then I'll be happy. When I have a kid, then life will have meaning. When I make my first million, then I'll really have accomplished something. But the reality is that a hunger for more will never be satisfied. There will always be another rung to climb or experience to have.

It's the person who can align their expectations with their current experiences that will be satisfied.

What you focus on is what you'll find. Look for the good.

Experiment

Question:

Who or what disappoints you? What expectations of yourself or others are leading to negative experiences, emotions, and outcomes (ie: disappointment, fighting, frustration, depression)?

Action:

Make a list of what expectations could be shifted—for your own good, and the good of others around you. It might feel like you're lowering your standards. But sometimes that's the very thing you must do to see any progress at all.

ATTITUDE

*"The mind is its own place, and in itself can make
a heaven of hell, a hell of heaven."*
—John Milton, Paradise Lost

When I turned 16 years old, my dad took me and a half dozen other men on a weekend trip for my birthday. These weren't kids from my volleyball team or from the neighborhood. These were friends that were closer to my dad's age.

My dad had a conviction. "There are too few markers in a person's life—not enough celebrating of the passages from one life stage to another. We should pause and be intentional about such things."

On the trip the men shared with me stories from their lives—things they found important, decisions they believed made the difference. We saw Braveheart in the theater—the ultimate "man movie." It was a memorable time. I was amazed that these men—heroes of mine, in some respects—all set aside this time just for me.

Lastly, my dad had asked these and couple dozen more men in my life to write me a letter about "becoming a man." I received about 30 letters in a notebook. I still have the notebook and I reflect on the letters periodically. I treasure the insights and encouragement of these wise men. There is something special about one generation of men welcoming younger men to their ranks.

One significant letter was written by my Uncle Joe. It was about attitude. The line that stood out the most to me in it was this: "The only thing you have control over is your attitude." Even at 16, I knew there was profound wisdom in these words.

There are a lot of hard things that happen in life. Some things we have no control over. Some things we brought upon ourselves. But either way, we can't change them. If we spend time thinking about the past, we inevitably become discouraged or guilt-ridden because, for most of us, there are things that happened in the past that we don't like. Things that happened to us, things we did, or opportunities we missed. Every year that goes by can serve as a reminder of our own imperfection and the corresponding consequences.

We should learn from our past, but not dwell on it. Similarly, if we think too much of our future, it is likely that we will become anxious or paranoid. "What if a certain scenario plays out? What if I run out of money? What if he leaves? What if they let me down? What if I fail?" Worrying about the future will only make us anxious and distracted.

We should plan for the future, but not obsess over it. When we regret the past or worry about the future there is one constant result: we miss the present. That's where attitude comes in. We can control where we put our minds. We can choose how we respond to any opportunity, set-back, or challenge.

Regardless of circumstances—past, present, or future—you can control your attitude today. You can control how you live right now. You can determine how you will respond no matter what the world throws at you—no matter how miserably you may fail.

To live this way means taking control of our minds. *Fix your thoughts on what is true and honorable and right. Think about things that are pure and lovely and admirable. Think about things that are excellent and worthy of praise.*[7]

This does not mean we live in denial of reality. The key is to keep our minds focused on the things that matter most, regardless of what's happening in the world around us.

Below is a scanned image of the piece of paper I have kept for years. Someone gave it to me long ago and I thought it to be profound.

---

7.   *Philippians 4:8*

ATTITUDE
BY
Charles Swindoll

"The longer I live, the more I realize the impact of attitude on life. **Attitude, to me, is more important than facts**. It is more important than the past, than education, than money, than circumstances, than failures, than successes, than what other people think or say or do. It is more important than appearance, giftedness or skill. **It will make or break a company... a church... a home... A TEAM.**

The remarkable thing is we have a choice every day regarding the attitude we will embrace for that day. **We cannot change our past... we cannot change the fact that people will act in a certain way. We cannot change the inevitable.** The only thing we can do is play on the one string we have, and that is our attitude... I am convinced that **life is 10% what happens to me and 90% how I react to it.** And so it is with you... **we are in charge of our attitudes.**"

Experiment

Question:

How would you describe your attitude right now? What kind of attitude would best-serve you for the rest of today?

Action:

Ask the person closest to you—spouse, family member, boyfriend, etc.—to describe their view of your recent attitude(s).

CRAZY WHEN IT MATTERS

"I've been touched by that bright fire, down to the root of my desire, while the smoke it rises higher, on crazy faith"
—Alison Krauss, Crazy Faith

Several days before we dispersed for Christmas break, I went with a group of college friends into downtown Los Angeles and we handed out food, blankets, and hot chocolate to homeless people. There were about twenty of us on this particular night in December. We always had a good time together, but on Skid-

Row? Privileged white kids exiting SUVs on Skid-Row with post-final-exam enthusiasm might have stood out…a little.

Our group broke up into teams of three to hand out everything we brought with us—jackets, blankets, diapers, canned food. An hour later, we met back at our rendezvous point. But no one knew where Chris was.

Apparently, Chris was last seen jetting down alleyways, looking for the not-so-obvious street-dwellers. Naturally, the rest of us became a little nervous.

We called him Smiley Chris. And the first thing we saw when he turned the corner were his pearly whites, beaming in the darkness of downtown. He was practically skipping. And he ws practically naked.

"Chris, where are your clothes," someone shouted?

"I gave them away! I've got plenty."

Bear in mind, it was about 50 degrees outside. (In Southern California, that's colder than a witch's… You get it.) I was cold, and I was not-so-generously still wearing my jacket.

Chris was wearing pants and a sleeveless undershirt. That's all. His shoes were gone. His socks were gone. His jacket was gone. His sweatshirt was gone. And his hat was gone. Chris ran out of blankets and food, he literally took the clothes off his back. The rest of us felt like the spoiled Americans we were, but we were inspired.

Thank you, Chris, for your smiling face and your shining example. You're crazy, but in the right way.

* * *

I have two younger bothers, Josh and Aaron. Josh is two years younger. So I was already at college when Josh was a senior in high school.

My senior year, I enjoyed a free period. I had taken more than enough classes and by having a free sixth period, I could go home early, get a jump on homework before practice, or pretend that I was doing something cooler than those things—like you do when you're a senior.

When Josh was senior, he could've had the same free period but he choose to fill it. He chose to be a teacher's aide in a Special Education class. "He wanted it to look good on his transcripts," some would say. Nope. Josh already knew he was playing football for a small college in the Midwest. But he didn't want to do what seniors in high school were doing. He wanted to make a difference.

I need to mention here that Josh was the starting quarterback at our high school his junior and senior years. Even though he was humble, he was especially recognizable on campus. So when he spent his free period working in the Special

Ed class, people noticed. People also noticed when Josh started pushing his new friends' wheelchairs around campus. In my four years at Claremont High school, I never saw a single football player pushing a wheelchair. But by the end of Josh's senior year, any given day, you could see a dozen different athletes pushing wheelchairs up the sidewalk slopes of that campus. Josh was having an impact.

After Josh went off to college, various football players and other athletes began using free periods to help in Special Ed classes. And the school continued to make a point of taking a bus of special needs students to a football game each season—something Josh helped initiate.

There were also a few relationships that Josh tried to maintain from college, and one in particular: Anna.

Anna didn't have use or control of her limps (quadriplegic). She was bound to a wheelchair, although I witnessed her pulling herself around on her rounded knees. It was difficult to understand Anna when she spoke. And she spoke plenty! She knew exactly what she wanted to say, but it didn't come out quite right. However, somehow Josh understood almost every word.

When Josh left for college, Anna would call the house and my mom would tell her that Josh was still away at school. Several times, despite Josh's freshman schedule and football demands, he would call Anna. She was thrilled out of her mind when he did.

Toward the end of the school year Josh talked to Anna about her upcoming graduation and her plans for after high school. Anna didn't have much in the way of plans. But she did have another idea. She asked Josh when he would be home. He said mid-May. It turned out that Claremont High School's prom was a week later, in late May. Josh was shocked she was even aware of prom. And then he was floored when she asked him if he would take her.

Anna…a girl who didn't own a fancy dress, couldn't comb her own hair, had never had a boyfriend, and obviously couldn't dance. She wanted to go to her senior prom. And she wanted to go with Josh—the star of last year's football team, and runner up for Homecoming King. Josh--the popular athlete who made it cool to care about kids with special needs in high school. Josh—her friend.

Put yourself in Josh's shoes. It's a challenging predicament. Neither Josh, I, or our other brother, Aaron, liked dances very much to begin with. Neither did we have any interest in going back to high school events—and being *that guy*—no matter how cute the younger girl might have been. But this was different. Very different.

Yet different didn't make it easy. In fact, to most 19-year-olds, this would've been *crazy*. Anna would not have other friends there, so she and Josh would be together the whole time. Josh would have to pay for a tux rental, the entry ticket, a flower, and make the long drive to the event (why are those lame dances at far away ballrooms?). All of that, and she might get there and be embarrassed and hate the whole experience. It was risky. And it would demand that Josh take his commitment to Anna to a whole new level—from teacher's aide and friend, to date.

But if you know my brother Josh, you know that he did the brave thing, the bold thing…the crazy thing. And luckily for me, I was home from college and got the privilege of driving.

We drove the big blue Suburban. Anna was dropped off at our home by her grandmother—her family situation was complicated. Anna looked beautiful. She was in a brand new dress. She had on make-up. My mom helped her put the finishing touches on her hair, and then Josh put the flower on her wrist. She was beaming. We hadn't left the house and this was already the best night of her life—I'm not exaggerating.

Anna's grandmother cried as she left, seeing Anna full of so much joy. My family didn't cry, but we all knew this was a sacred event—the kind of thing that makes you a better person just by proximity.

We put the wheelchair in the back of the Suburban and Josh carried her to her seat. We drove the hour to the event (I think it was in Long Beach). We listened to the radio stations that Anna liked to listen to. I kept peeking back in my rearview mirror to see the expressions on her face. The hour actually went by fast, as we had fun making Anna laugh and reminiscing about funny high school things.

We pulled up to the ballroom about 30 minutes late. I parked the big blue ride along the curb and had a direct view down the walkway to the big entrance doors. After jumping out to grab Anna's wheelchair and to give my brother a hug, I sat in the car and waited…and watched.

Josh pushed Anna the 50 yards to the entrance. I could see him produce the prom tickets, but I don't think the person at the door remembered to take them. From my seat I could literally see jaws drop. Josh, last year's football star, was back. And his date…Anna—beaming from ear to ear.

Several faculty members hurried to open the doors. I saw them try to make extra room while motioning to others to pay attention.

By the time Anna's wheelchair crossed the threshold, a large group of students had already stopped dancing and were lining up to greet them, like a human tunnel on either side of the aisle-way.

In the history of Claremont High School, there have been a handful of students who went on to become celebrities—actors, professional athletes. And schools like boasting that kind of thing. I, too, like to think that my four years at that school left some kind of positive legacy and made a difference in some people's lives. But nothing that I've ever personally witnessed can compare with that night, that prom, Anna, and my brother Josh. Tears streamed down my face as I drove away, knowing that that night, the world became a better place.

If you were to go to Claremont high school on a Friday in the fall, you'll probably see some large varsity football players in their game jerseys, pushing wheelchairs around the campus. And you'll know that started because one guy cared about people and did something unusual. He did something a little bit crazy (giving up a free period), a little bit counter-cultural (hanging out with Special Ed students instead of just his popular friends), and something that will not soon be forgotten. He gave a precious girl the memory of her life.

Josh and Anna gave me, my family, and a high school, inspiration that there is a different and better way to live.

I wonder how many amazing moments you and I have missed out on by not being willing to be a little bit crazy.

Experiment

Question:
In the past, what has prevented you from doing "crazy" things that would have a positive impact on someone else? Fear? Popular opinion? Comfort?

Action:
Do something out of your comfort zone today or tomorrow. Something out of the ordinary, risky, bold. Do something for the benefit of someone else.

Share your stories at **myneardeathexperiment.com**

ME TOO

*"Could a greater miracle occur than to look
through each other's eyes for an instant?"*
—Henri David Thoreau

There was as boy named Tommy—probably 16—who sat in a YMCA by himself one day. Tommy had been in a boating accident that resulted in the amputation of most of his left leg. His parents made him go to the YMCA twice a week after school, just like he used to do. But now Tommy hated it. He could not do the activities he once did. He felt like everyone looked at him and felt sorry for him. The day I saw him, he was sitting alone.

A cycling class let out and the members walked from the room towards the exit. A man coming out of the class walked with a quick pace and an almost-normal stride. Tommy didn't see the man approaching, but the man saw Tommy.

"Hi. I'm Dave," the man offered.

"Hi," was all Tommy responded.

"When was your accident?" Dave asked Tommy.

"It's been eight months."

"Do you work out while you're here?" Dave asked, pressing Tommy's comfort level.

"No…not much motivation any more. And, obviously, I can't do much," Tommy said, making eye contact with Dave for the first time and motioning toward his legs.

"I get it," Dave said. Then he lifted the right leg of his sweat pants, revealing an aluminum rod.

"It's been eight years for me," Dave continued. "It gets easier. I promise. How about you and I work out together next time?"

Not only did Tommy's countenance change, his whole perspective changed in that moment. He wasn't alone.

"One of the greatest diseases is to be nobody to anybody."
—Mother Teresa

* * *

When I went through my quarter-life crisis of 2006 I stumbled my way into counseling. Certainly, I have issues. I obviously needed to learn how to express some things under the surface that didn't get discussed in my family. So…who can I pay that will acutely probe my soul and help me heal?

In addition to counseling, I attended a conference, met with pastors, prayed with friends, and read a couple books. I was desperate. I wanted to speed through this season of disruptive agony as quickly as possible and get back on the road to world-domination. Back on the path toward making more of me.

Here's the problem: I was starting from *selfish.*

We're all born with Selfish Syndrome. And when selfish people go through pain and trauma, our culture tell us to do what? *Focus more on ourselves!* "Go get counseling. Try retail therapy. Go on vacation. Process your feelings. Take care of you. Enjoy some me-time." This advice is not necessarily evil or wrong. But I'd argue that in most cases it compounds our pre-existing problem: our self-centeredness.

There is obvious danger in telling self-serving people to focus more on themselves. Staring inward is necessary for personal awareness, but destructive when it becomes our obsession. That's because, in essence, *you* become your obsession. And we wonder why people are so self-absorbed and why relationships are failing. Selfishness is the primary killer of relationships.

And here's the interesting thing: I don't have to convince you. You immediately think of all the self-centered people in your life, and you agree. The people who only call you when they need something. The people who ask questions only to have others ask them the question back. The people that totally miss social queues and have no sensitively to their surroundings. They have a difficult time seeing beyond themselves.

That's the easy part. Yes, you're surrounded by selfish people. And if that's the conclusion you finish with, you're screwed. Because you can't change them. As much as you'd like to; and as right as you are…you'll never make someone else less selfish. And that's okay.

Here's why it's okay: Because the real problem is you.

It's actually *your* selfishness that's killing your relationships.

The story goes that a British newspaper invited several influential thinkers of a previous generation to weigh-in publicly on the topic, "What is wrong with the world?" They received numerous responses, but only one has become a famously insightful indictment of our human condition:

> *"Dear Sir:*
> *Regarding your article 'What's Wrong with the World?'*
> *I am.*
> *Yours truly,"*
> —G.K. Chesterton

As badly as you want it, as sincere as you may be…you will never change someone else. They have to choose to change. The only person you can change is YOU. And you must. Because the truth is, your selfishness is your biggest problem.

* * *

You are blinded to your selfishness because of your woundedness.

It's your pain, not your pride, that blinds you. It's hurt you've experienced that causes you to put up defenses of self-protection. The problem is that self-protection becomes a prison of self-centeredness.

Selfishness keeps us focused on our own issues. Selfishness keeps us too busy to notice the pain of others we pass by.

But love…love notices, stops, and relates.

Do you know why support groups like AA, Celebrate Recovery and others are successful? Sure, the material is good. But do you know why it really works? Because we all need to know we're not alone.

1. There is a Creator-God ("Higher Power") who actually cares and is mysteriously involved in our lives.
2. There are other people who can relate to our situation, empathize with our pain, and encourage us to keep on going.

As human beings, there are no new issues. Everything is common on some level. None of us are alone.

Writer Anne Lamott says that the most powerful sermon in the world is just two words: "Me, too."

Experiment

Question:

How is self-focus impacting your relationships? Is there someone you need to reach out to—someone going through pain, and you can relate?

Action:

Look for the lonely and isolated today. Look for your "me too" moment.

At our core, we're all the same. Choose love.

> *Above all, love each other deeply,*
> *because love covers over a multitude of sins.*
> —1 Peter 4:8

BYE BYE PRIDE

Pride leads to destruction; a proud attitude brings ruin.
—Proverbs 16:18 (NCV)

I was well on my way. At 26, I had a been a collegiate volleyball player and captain, had spoken to large audiences on three continents, had a literary agent shopping my first book, and I was married to a model. That all seems good on the surface, but I wasn't content.

If you would have asked me what my greatest fear was, I would've have responded immediately: "Not reaching my potential."

Growing up the oldest of three boys and eleven grandkids, I was the example-setter in the family. I started being selected as the captain of all my sports team, and the pressure I felt on the inside to be someone special continued to mount.

A slogan I remember growing up was, "people are always watching you." I'm not sure if it was the mantra of my parents or pastor, but it haunted me. Those words rang in my head, keeping me from outward "sins," but driving me toward inward pride and shame.

After all, I was pretty good at being good. I didn't do the big "sins." I didn't get in trouble for "bad" things. So my pride protected me from my inner struggles and insecurities.

* * *

When I graduated from college, the obvious next step was to get married and get a job. And the obvious person to marry was someone *freaking hot* who shared my same spiritual convictions. Everything else will take care of itself, right?

For my age, 22 at the time I got married, I was mature in some obvious ways—attitude, outlook, work ethic, social skills—but also quite immature emotionally.

Growing up the All-American kid that others looked up to, I felt a lot of pressure, though I didn't recognize it at the time. I didn't realize it, but I was performing with my life. I was committed to upholding the standards of my family and my faith. I was determined to be an example worth following, a team captain worth voting for, and a brother worthy of admiration. But who was I, really?

My life was a confusing mix of genuine faith and a thick layer of self-protecting pride. I was afraid of failure from a very young age. More than that, I was afraid I would not reach my full potential—that ambiguous future self that's more awesome and has more accolades than my current self. I didn't know when or how I'd ever reach that glowing pedestal in my mind where I was generally heralded as "great."

The pressure I constantly put on myself to perform was normal for me. But in marriage, it was quickly apparent that my "other half" was not interested in participating in my pressure-filled pursuit of being somebody. We fought like cats and dogs. I seemed hypocritical to her, she was rebellious to me. I grew cold toward her. I was critical and difficult to live with. But, to me, she was only getting a taste of the inner pressure and expectation that I put on myself everyday.

Over time, she grew more frustrated and I became more callous. Life and marriage were not turning out as I had planned. "Really, God, this is my life?"

Combine increasing discontentment with my hidden life of pride and pressure to look the part and what do you get? A pornography addiction. It's secret, it's selfish, and it's self-sufficient. And the more hopeless I became in my marriage, the more I gave into addiction.

I hid the severity and progression of problem for a long time. And I thought she was wrong for leaving. After all, "I didn't commit the *big* sins!"

Pride promises self-protection, but it delivers self-deception and self-destruction.

I made her feel like her issues were worse than mine. The truth was that my issues killed our marriage.

Something broke in me one day when I arrived home and the closet was bare. She had emptied all her things. She was actually leaving.

Rock-bottom is an ugly friend. It might be just what you need, but, by all means, avoid it if you can.

I lay on the ground outside our closet for 30 hours. I crawled to the bathroom to pee. That's it.

After sharing this story with a gathering of men, one guy approached me and said he could relate.

"I've been more depressed than you," he said.

"Really," I inquired? Do tell.

"Yeah. I lay on the ground for 48 hours, and I didn't even get up to go the bathroom. I just went all over myself, right there on the floor."

"Uh…ok. You win."

* * *

You'd think that experience—and the resulting end of a marriage—would have dealt my pride a fatal blow. But pride is resilient.

The year that followed I continued to struggle with hurt and frustration. Why me? Why divorce? Why such devastating humiliation? I didn't deserve this! I was trying to be good (for the most part). Everyone has issues. Why did mine have to cost me so much? Why couldn't I have just been an idiot in college when I was single—and done whatever I wanted?

Still in the thick of my crisis and confusion, I got a call from my mom.

"You'll feel better, and have a healthier perspective, if you get the focus off yourself and serve other people."

I took her advice and chose the YMCA. At the time, I was living in a community where the YMCA was the coolest work-out facility around. It was first-class, yet also catered to the less fortunate (with scholarships, etc.). I had an acquaintance who worked there, so I asked if they needed help. The next day I found myself at the front desk, greeting members, and handing out towels…in a red t-shirt.

A red t-shirt! That was a huge challenge for me. So were obnoxious members who whined about silly things and talked down to people in red t-shirts. "I don't have to be here," I wanted to say when spoken to condescendingly. Again, part of the journey I wouldn't have chosen.

Before long, the journey took a turn, and I began to see some purpose in my pride-swallowing role. I learned about the Y's desire to help their members grow in spirit, mind, and body. I reflected on my previous experience writing and creating campaigns for churches. I proposed an idea.

"What if we create a campaign at the Y around spirit, mind, body? What if I wrote a book of daily encouragements and we took a month to emphasize healthy life-changes in each of these areas?"

They liked the idea. In fact, they paid for and distributed 10,000 copies of the book.

And it worked. People actually liked it. Members asked for additional books, so I printed more, selling another 1,500, just word of mouth.

More important than any numbers is that fact that it actually helped people. I received letters and emails that year thanking me for the book…my first book. And that book was the foundation that gave me confidence, credibility, and experience for this book. (Since then, the book as been republished as *40 Days to a New You.*)

There is a bigger plan. There is purpose behind temporary pain. A little humility goes a long way. But you might have to wear a red t-shirt and kill your pride before the next opportunity presents itself.

Pride asks, "Why me?" Humility takes the focus *off* of me.

Some people have wrongly believed that humility is about denying your strengths or taking a passive backseat. That's not humility at all.

Humility doesn't cause you to think less of yourself. In humility, you think of yourself less.

Experiment

Question:

What pain has pride caused in your life?

Experiment:

Make a list of ways your pride affects you and others. If you're not sure, ask someone close to you (who is brave, but not abusive).

SPEAKER FOR THE DEAD

"I grew dissatisfied with the way that we use our funerals to revise the life of the dead, to give the dead a story so different from their actual life... We edit them, we make them into a person much easier to live with than the person who actually lived... I thought that a more appropriate funeral would be to say, honestly, what that person was and what that person did...To understand who a person really was, what his or her life really meant, the speaker for the dead would have to explain their self-story—what they meant to do, what they actually did, what they regretted, what they rejoiced in. That's the story that we never know." — Orson Scott Card, of his science-fiction novel, Speaker for the Dead

I've been a "speaker for the dead." I've given eulogies, shared memories, or played a role in funerals. And I'll tell you this: There's a big difference between a typical funeral and a celebration of life. A funeral feels like a funeral—it's all about the loss and no legacy. There is grieving, but almost in a hopeless sense. People share some stories or a memory, but there's often anger, fear, and uncertainty.

I recently conducted a funeral ceremony for a 50-something gentleman who worked at a large department store. I had never met him. But I quickly learned that he had battled his share of demons and addictions. By his death, he had estranged himself from his entire family. His ex-wife wanted nothing to do with the funeral. No one in his family attended. Only about 30 people who worked with him at the department store showed up. They were shaken. They clearly didn't spend much time considering their own mortality, and this man's death shocked them—most had no idea how to process the event.

By the end, we created some levity and hope. I even invited people to share what they appreciated about their friend. At first, crickets. Then one brave soul. "This one time, on break…" Nothing that will make Wikipedia, but it got the ball rolling. Several others shared heart-felt sentiments. It was short but kind. They did their best to speak for the dead.

* * *

When my wife's mother died the news shook the community. Kimi wasn't gregarious or particularly out-going, but she was genuine, full of joy and love. You wouldn't have thought she had a broad network of influence, but over a thousand people turned out for the celebration of her life. It was jaw-dropping. Standing room only. The family was overwhelmed with pride and gratitude. I had the privilege of giving the eulogy. In a way, it was the easiest sharing I've ever done. Her life spoke for itself. And it still speaks—through the lasting legacy that Kimi has left on many.

"The legacy we leave is not just in our possessions, but in the quality of our lives. What preparations should we be making now? The greatest waste in all of our earth, which cannot be recycled or reclaimed, is our waste of the time that God has given us each day." —Billy Graham

The journey of this book aims at increasing the quality of your life. Reflecting on the reality of death brings clarity to life. By the end of this book, you'll be a Death User.

A Death User is someone who leverages death for the sake of life. A Death User has no more fear of death. Death is what it is. It will come. It will come for people that you love. And, one day, it will come for you.

As it's been said, "everyone dies, but not everyone truly lives."

There is no need to fear death. You have too much *living* to do.

Instead of fearing death, you're going to *use* death. You will use the mysterious reality of death to your benefit—you'll let death inspire life. You'll prepare for future days by making the most of this single day—today.

Just as responsible people create wills for the sake of their loved ones—to alleviate chaos after they pass—so you and I must stare certain death in the face, long before our eyes go dark. We'll choose, intentionally, to live a life we're proud of—a life well-lived.

At the end of this book, I'm going to help you design a Death Contract. You've heard of a Living Will? Well your Death Contract will embody your *will to live*— to live the life that makes the most of who you are and the time you have.

Yesterday is gone. Tomorrow is uncertain. But today you can use death and make the most of your life.

Experiment:

Question:
If you were asked to be the "Speaker for the Dead" for one person, whose life would make you most proud to celebrate? What makes that person's life significant?

Action:
List the three most important things you hope others will say about you when you die.

If we are not growing, we are regressing. If we are not changing for the better, we are changing for the worse.

YOULOGY
[eulogy]

The Real You
You will consistently live in alignment with what you believe to be true about yourself.

"People who say they don't ca what people think are usually desperate to have people think they don't care what people thi
—George Carlin

THE SHADOW LIFE

"Character is like a tree and reputation like a shadow. The shadow is what we think of it; the tree is the real thing."
—Abraham Lincoln

Remember the movie Peter Pan? Peter had a shadow problem. Sometimes, the shadow would ignore Peter's movements and just does its own thing.

We all have shadows. And by "shadow" I mean the darker part of self—the part that moves like us, looks like us...but when we're not looking, it acts out on its own.

As my quarter-life-crisis was in full swing I was caught off-guard by the comment of a good friend. I was still at the stage where I was expecting sympathy or a pep-talk. After all, I was losing everything—wife, house, car, dog, dream... Instead Ty said, "You know, I'm kinda glad this is happening to you. I feared you were on your way to becoming another prominent Christian asshole."

I think that what he meant was an arrogant ministry person who leveraged their abilities to make a name for themselves, instead of truly, humbly serving others. That's not who I wanted to be. But looking back, I see how I let myself be confused about what I was doing and why.

And the reality is, there is still a Shadow Life trying to high-jack my efforts and attitudes today. And Ty has his own Shadow Life to keep in check. And you do too.

* * *

There is a life inside of me that wants to burst free and live well, strong, confident. Sometimes it does. But often it doesn't. It seems there's something holding me back. A *resistance* to the Good Life. It can feel like a wet towel around my shoulders. It has also seemed as if a dark cloud hovered above me, blocking out the sun.

On good mornings I wake up and it's not there. Other days I can outrun it and find green fields and warm sun. But there have been days when I feel like I'm a lesser version of myself.

In my own personal journey, I've been greatly blessed. But I've also been greatly burdened. I've been forced to learn—and I'm still learning—how not to...

- fear your own potential
- rest on your talents
- hide your weaknesses
- just try harder

Instead I'm learning how to...

- embrace who I am
- tap into the supernatural
- live honestly out of weakness
- surrender

That's not sexy, but it's real. And it's good.

Light exposes our shadows. *All those who do evil hate the light, and will not come into the light for fear that their deeds will be exposed.*[1]

The Shadow Life mixes us up and messes with our minds. It gets to us to settle for lesser experiences, promises bigger payoffs, and never delivers. It can take the form of apathy or ambition, anxiousness, or aggression.

The Shadow Life will manipulate your passions and lead you to addictions. The Light is scary, but it's on your side. More light...less shadow.

Experiment

Question:
Shadows exist where there are barriers to light. What are the barriers to light in your life?

Action:
Define your Shadow Life.

"Be more concerned with your character than your reputation, because your character is what you really are, while your reputation is merely what others think you are." —John Wooden

UNCOVERED

"Turn your face to the sun and the shadows fall behind you."
—Maori Proverb

I had a friend in college who was obsessed with her physical appearance. She came by her obsession honestly. Her mom gave top priority to physical and material things. And it's likely that her mom's mom did the same. We all have roots to our dysfunction.

1.   *John 3:20*

But my friend—call her Katie—was the most extreme that I knew. She literally wouldn't let another human being see her without make-up. Even her roommate couldn't lift the veil. Katie would wait until the light turned off, then she would go to the bathroom, remove her make-up, and come back to bed. While asleep, she wore an eye-cover that wrapped half her face. In the morning, she was always the first one up and would go straight to the bathroom. Think about the anxiety of being a slave to this pressure!

But, ironically for Katie, break-through came in Mexico. Mexico was Katie's crisis and her awakening.

She went down with a group of college student-friends on a do-good exposure trip. It's the kind of thing socially-minded students do when spring break party trips seem too small.

What Katie didn't know, was that she'd be living alone with a Mexican family, in their home, without her friends and with no modern comforts. The family that Katie stayed with didn't have running water. And the water they did have was barely enough to boil, clean, and drink. You've likely heard of people—many middle class Americans—living month-to-month. Well this family lived meal-to-meal. They were fully aware of the fact that they might not eat dinner any given night. And yet they made sure Katie was the first to fill her plate.

When Katie saw her Mexico living environment she panicked. She didn't understand the severity of the circumstances when she signed up. She knew she was in trouble. She anxiously analyzed how many days she could manipulate her appearance without the luxury of her beauty rituals.

After 24 hours, she was holding it together on the outside, but was terrified on the inside. Yet something else was happening, too.

The family that Katie was living with had a 15-year-old daughter. She was pretty, in a simple way. She had a beautiful smile that boasted inner confidence and a gratitude for the life she knew. The girl had two dresses, two blouses, and one pair of khaki pants...and no make-up.

One night, the girl and Katie were sitting on Katie's temporary cot in the family's paper-thin home. "You're so pretty," the girl told Katie.

"No," Katie, responded, void of false humility. "*You* are pretty. You're beautiful."

"No I'm not," the girl said as she grinned and looked away. "I don't even have make-up."

Now, to this day, Katie can't quite articulate what happened. But in that Mexican casa, something changed for Katie.

It was not a near death experience; it became a Significant Learning Moment. Mexico was the *experiment*. Make-up was the sacrifice. A 15-year-old girl was the surprise instructor. And Katie found herself on the verge of change.

There was a light that sparked inside. A light that exposed something hidden; something covered. Katie's soul was stirring. She realized on that cot that her temporary living situation was not temporary for her generous hosts. This was all they had, all they needed. And it was enough. In fact, it was beautiful.

Katie is a beautiful girl. Yet she was afraid that people would think less of her if they saw the "real her." Katie's transformation was not instantaneous, but the next day, she wore a little less cover-up. Today, Katie wears light make-up about half the time. She is confident and free.

* * *

My crisis was not Mexico. My crisis was divorce.

You can't hide divorce. A crisis like that forces you into the light, whether you like it or not. And I certainly did not.

When you're married, someone else sees behind the curtain. They know what you can be like behind closed doors. They know how cold and closed off you can be. They know the way you talk when you're angry and unfiltered. They know all too well the habits that you've not been able to break. And at 25, I was married to someone who had had enough and blew the whistle. It was my most devastating season of life, by far. I had lived for my reputation. I had a PhD in image-management. I had ascended to leadership and status. I was liked by many, respected by more. And I was on my way to "making something of myself." And then it all came crashing down.

When something like that happens it's not only a matter of coming into the light; it's worse than that. It's like a spotlight when you feel naked, pasty, and fat.

When you're down and out, and in the grip of humiliation, certain types of people like to bring little flashlights of their own. They like to try and expose more and exaggerate the process. Some like to feel that they can relate to you, and then they smoother you with their own insecurities. And—to a certain degree—you just have to take it!

If I were to run, deny, or dismiss, I'd just have been prolonging the inevitable. Because—they don't tell you this in seminars—humility requires some manner of humiliation. And the longer you fight it, the more arrogant you become. And the more arrogant you become, the more messy it is when fan blades fling your feces.

In my case, I wanted to justify myself, clarify the facts, and set things straight. My instinct was self-preservation. I thought my ex was irrational and overreacting. Later I could see that she wasn't. And looking back, I don't know if anything less would've gotten my attention.

I had learned to depend on the darkness to manage my image. But you can only walk in darkness for so long before you get lost. Jesus said, *Those who walk in the dark do not know where they are going. Put your trust in the light...* Walking in darkness you stumble around and cause damage—to yourself and others.

My crisis felt like it was killing me. But it was actually giving me new life. It was bringing me out of the darkness and into the Light.

When you live concerned about your approval rating, you inevitably live in the dark. Why? Because we all know, without our make-up, there are some people who will think we're ugly. On some level, all of us fear being totally honest, completely vulnerable, and utterly known.

If we're really known, we will surely be rejected. I've been rejected in a real way, but life goes on. That's not the end of the story.

Today, I'm living a better life. My challenges have made me stronger. My dreams are becoming reality. And I'm trying less, enjoying more.

Strangely, I'm healthier and more confident as a result of being "uncovered."

Katie killed the cover-up, too. She began to let people see her without make-up and she grew in strength and contentment because of it. That might seem silly to you, but to Katie, it was almost life and death. She literally didn't know what would happen, and if she could live with the potential rejection.

One reason we don't bring our struggles, fears, and failures into the light is because we fear we'll lose the respect of others and be disqualified for something. That's why pastors are among the loneliest men alive. They fear that if you and I knew their thoughts and their secrets that you'd reject them. And it happens all the time.

But rejection is not from God. Jesus said, *"I have come to save the world and not to judge it"*[2]. If you come into the Light, God will never reject you. No matter what.

You can never be disqualified. Certain people who still struggle with their own darkness might tell you otherwise. They might fire you. They might ask you not to come back to their thing. They might tell you not to date their daughter. Yes, they might reject you completely. But it's only because they still in the dark themselves.

We're all the same. We're all prone to cover-up. We all have darkness in us. And we all need the Light to shine into our lives and save us from the darkness that we've grown to accept as normal. It's not normal. There's a better way.

---

2. *John 12:47*

Experiment

Question:

Ask yourself, "Am I a safe person that others can trust? Or do others feel judged by me?" Others will feel judged by you if:

- You're not honest about your own issues;
- You're always giving and not receiving advice; or
- They hear you talk critically of others.

Action:

Write down in your journal the thing you feel most anxious and insecure about—the thing you're most afraid of having "uncovered." Circle it. Now put a bold line through it. Freedom is coming.

iCAN

"Whether you think you can or you can't—you're right."
—Henry Ford

The NFL Football season of 2011 was an unusual year of football. It was the year the Green Bay Packers nearly went undefeated as defending Super Bowl champions. It was the year their quarterback, Aaron Rodgers, played like a video game icon—near perfect. And it was the year of Tim Tebow.

I have never seen so much hype about a single player. Not Joe Montana, not LeBron James, not even Michael Jordon. "Tebowing" became a verb: kneeling on one knee with an arm to the head, praying. Every fourth story on ESPN involved Tim Tebow. Some called him the most polarizing figure in the history of professional sports. Why? Because of his bold faith and what seemed like a lack of elite NFL quarterback fundamentals. But Tebow won games—six of his first seven games. He was famous for struggling for three quarters, then staging monumental comebacks in the fourth quarter to win. Rational sports reporters began to ask themselves serious questions about the role of Divine intervention for this athlete with an obviously strong faith in God, giving thanks to "my Lord and Savior, Jesus Christ," in every interview.

Does God mettle in professional football outcomes? I doubt it. But there is one other reality that I think explains the phenomenon of 2011 as well as anything: Tim Tebow believed he could win. In any and every situation, regardless of how poorly he'd played to that point... He believed he had what it took to get the job done.

Throughout that first season, Tim listened to critique, but ignored critics. He listened to feedback to refine his game, but he wouldn't believe anyone who told him that he didn't belong in the NFL. He seemed to align with a philosophy that I hold:

Criticism is like chewing gum. You chew it, test the favor, but never swallow it.

Tebow believed at his core that he could win in the NFL. And so, in his inaugural season as a starter, with the odds stacked against him, he did just that...he won games...and led his team to the playoffs and a playoff victory.

Whether you believe you can or you can't, you're right.

Let me ask you a few questions: Can you run a marathon? Can you start your own business? Can you change the life of an orphan? How about feed an entire orphanage?

The answer to all of these questions, and infinitely more, is YES. Yes, YOU CAN.

Do you have the resources to feed the orphanage at this moment? Perhaps not. But if you really want to, you could get the resources. Do you have the skill to start a business? You could learn. Do you have the stamina for the marathon this weekend? I don't. But if you trained, you could do it.

Begin with this simple belief: *You can.* You can change. You can grow and improve. You can finish this book and be better for it. You can walk in the ways that were meant for you even before you were born.[3]

Simple belief: You can.

And now, a simple commitment: *Kill doubt.*

One of things you'll learn through Your Near Death Experiment is that *some things have to die.* Doubt is one of those things.

Doubt is often derived from fear. We fear disappointment and discouragement so we don't try. We fear humiliation so we don't risk. Our doubts can make us unstable, uncommitted, and insecure.[4]

You might be plagued with an unhelpful inner voice. Any inner voice that fuels insecurity, self-doubt, lack of confidence, or shame is an unhelpful voice. Kill it.

"I wish it were that easy," you might say. It's not easy. Not much of value is easy. But it's simple. And you can.

---

3.   *Ephesians 2:10, Jeremiah 29:11*

4.   *James 1:6*

This is not the time to psycho-analyze your entire life and discover the root of all insecurity, self-doubt, and shame. Instead, we're just going to start with the present moment and move *forward* from here.

As of today, you no longer have time for self-doubt. Every time a self-critical, negative thought comes to your mind, you reject. Every time that old tape plays in your mind, you destroy it. Every time that voice pipes up and tries to make you feel small, you shut it up. Every time. And if you fail and give way to doubt, don't listen to the condemning voices that tell you to give up, that you can't do this. Just start again. You're making progress. You're headed in the right direction.

> *"God is more interested in your direction*
> *than He is in your perfection."*
> —Jack Hayford

At 19-years-old I was invited to play for the USA Junior National Volleyball team in Colorado Springs. I knew it was a great honor, but I was scared to go. I was plagued by self-doubt. My first instinct is to blame my college coach. He certainly did not help my confidence. But it was my own fault. I allowed doubt to creep in. I listened to critical voices in my head, and I got insecure: "I'm not one of the best players in the country. I don't even start for my college team. I'm tired of angry coaches. I'm not confident enough to perform at my best."

Still, I went Colorado. I tried to talk myself into confidence leading up to our match versus Canada. When got into the game, things were going well and we were winning. Then, something happened. I was the setter, and a hitter got blocked and looked at me like it was my fault. My insecurity kicked in. Maybe it was my fault. Maybe I don't belong here. As the game got away from us I got quieter, more timid, and more insecure.

Frustrated and embarrassed, I wanted to be alone that night. If I couldn't win at that level, did it mean I had reached my peak as an athlete? Were all the other guys better than me with brighter futures? Why couldn't I control my thoughts and overcome fears?

I called my dad that night. I told him what had happened. He was calm, and he confidently shared with me a perspective-changing truth.

"So what you're telling me is that for 15 of the 25 points you held your own with the best volleyball players your age in the world, is that right?"

"Uh… yeah, I guess. But then I struggled."

"Fine. You struggled. So, now your next goal is to play at that level for more than 15 points. It's simple. They invited you because you belong there. Today, you proved that you belong there. Now you just get to *improve!*"

It's basic. It's simple. And it's true. Sometimes we need someone else to help us see the slightest perspective shift that could change everything.

I CAN play at that level. I did. I didn't fail. I just had some improving to do. Kill doubt. Shift your perspective. Replace a negative with a positive. Think on things that are true, right, good, helpful...[5] Not just right now. Every time a negative thought enters your mind, kill it. Then replace it with a better thought.

I know, you've tried before. But I don't care, and neither should you. Today is the first day of the rest of your life. Everyday you wake up there is a newness in the air. There has never been a day like today. Today is a day for beginning new normals. Today, YOU CAN.

Experiment

Question:
What do you need to believe that you CAN do today?

Action:
Write down the lies of self-doubt and discouragement that are getting in your way. Choose a new thought—perhaps a bible verse, quote, or inspiring phrase—that will replace the negative thought every time it pops into your mind. Write down the new idea and put it in a place where you'll constantly see it.

My 19-year-old example...

Doubt: I don't belong here. I'm not good enough.
Truth: I can play at this high level. And I will improve daily.

"When you improve a little each day, eventually big things occur...Don't look for the quick, big improvement. Seek the small improvement one day at a time. That's the only way it happens—and when it happens, it lasts." —John Wooden

UNEARNED TROPHIES

"Tis' better to live your own life imperfectly than to imitate someone else's perfectly."
—Elizabeth Gilbert (Eat, Pray, Love)

5.   *Phil 4:8*

Paradox: *Two seemingly opposing ideas that are both mysteriously true or accurate.*

Here's a paradox at the center of universe: There's no one like you. And… we're all the same.

Every living thing is unique in its creation. (God has no limits to His creativity.) And, every living thing is connected, with much in common.

My DNA is one-of-a kind. My humanness is shared by billions.

Our very existence is an incredible paradox. Some scientists believe that our universe was created out of a "big bang." And while this blast is said to have created everything in our world, galaxy, universe—incomprehensibly large and elaborate—its beginning was absurdly small. All of creation was made from seemingly nothing. *"Let there be light!"*

And then there's you. I know your life might not seem very miraculous today, but it is. Some of us were told that our conception was a "mistake." That our parents weren't trying. Some unfit parents have even gone so far as to regret their children…abort their children…abuse their children.

No life is a "mistake." All lives are miracles. There may be accidental parents, but there are no accidental souls.

The pregnant sixteen-year-old on the reality TV show is content with her 15 minutes of fame, but she seems to be missing out on the miracle of her journey. Just ask the millions of women who try month after month to conceive—charts on the wall, thermometer beside the bed…husband wondering if he can rise to the occasion yet, again…Science can work wonders. But I've been in the offices of multiple infertility clinics and I have had conservations with numerous families who've leveraged the best of science to conceive a child. Nearly every single one of them still reach a humble place of acknowledging that God, somehow, is the Giver of life. Life is a miracle that our smartest specialists still can't quite explain. And yet *here you are*…alive.

Your life is another life—just like the other billions of lives. And, your life is totally unique.

* * *

For many children like me across America, the 80's and 90's were "The AYSO Era." The American Youth Soccer Organization coordinates soccer leagues for children. I played in AYSO leagues for several seasons as a kid. The AYSO slogan, at least in my day, was "everybody wins." To their credit, they wanted every child to feel like a winner and to have a great experience playing soccer. So at the end of every season, no matter how many games you won or lost, each player received a trophy. The gesture was nice, but let's be honest, not everyone deserves a trophy for soccer. I was kind of a competitive kid, so a trophy after a losing season was like squeezing lemon juice in a paper cut. I remember giving away one of my AYSO trophies as a white elephant gift at Christmas. The unlucky gift recipient deserved it as much as my soccer team.

Self-Esteem: Feelings about yourself
Self-Image: Picture of yourself

AYSO was part of a larger trend toward building the self-esteem of kids. I'm a huge proponent of building self-esteem. But it has to be real; otherwise it actually accomplishes the opposite. Artificial encouragement is confusing and harmful to a kid's self-image. And we're not preparing anyone for the realities of life.

Imagine a 21-year-old with lots of AYSO trophies on their shelf floundering in their first real job at a local coffee shop. (This probably isn't difficult for you to imagine.) They consistently mess up coffee orders, they can't keep up with the pace, and they don't get along with their co-workers. "But at least I'm here," they argue in their own defense. In this person's mind, being present is supposed to be enough for trophies and rewards.

But it isn't.

The reality is that many of us who participated in the "everybody wins" era have decent feelings about ourselves, but we have confused or unclear *pictures* of ourselves. We're confused about who we are and what we should do about it. We struggle for years trying to figure out how to make our mark on the world, asking, "When is my turn? When can I lead? When will someone recognize how special I am?"

But there's hope.

You are special. You are unique. You do deserve trophies. But something else must come first.

Focusing exclusively on your uniqueness—on yourself—is a road to ruin. There is a certain order of things. Before we realize the expression of our individuality, there is one great life lesson that must be learned:

We're all the same.

We all share the great common bond of humanity. We all are dependent on a Creator for our very life. None of us is the source of our own origin. No one human life has more intrinsic value than another. All of us were created equal. All of us were created by a Creator.[6]

---

6. *Gen 1-2*

It doesn't matter your race, your creed, your ethnicity, your education, your talent, your aptitude…you are just as valuable as every human being alive. And every human being alive is just as valuable as you.

You may come from a moral background or a rebellious background. You may have made all the right choices or all the wrong ones. You may know the "important" people or the "insignificant" people. You might be on the fast track or the slow track.

You might have grown up with your parents or others telling you that you are special, a winner, a leader, someone of significance. You might have been set apart from your peers as the "golden boy" or girl. Or, you might have grown up having others tell you that you'll never amount to anything, you'll never add up, you won't achieve significance. Either way—for either person—there is freedom in this message: We're all the same.

No outside influence can diminish your God-given value. We all share a common Creator, a common humanity, and incredible worth. We're each gloriously priceless. We have the same value as the President. And the same value as the malnourished child on the other side of the world who won't survive this day.

* * *

Every kid deserves a trophy, but not for soccer. Part of losing at soccer is learning. Learning that there are weakness to address. Learning that there are other sports that might be a more natural fit. Learning that teams are essential for life, and scores are critical for progress.

Several of my college volleyball teammates who didn't end up being the stars of the team actually went on to be quite successful in business. They applied their competitive drive to a career that was a better fit.

My friend Graeme was a collegiate swimmer. He was good there, but didn't have the success he wanted. After college he discovered beach volleyball. At 6'8" he moved out to Huntington Beach and has quickly become a great volleyball player. He found his "dream job" that allows him to coach, mentor younger athletes, and play volleyball.

Christian Okoya was recruited from Nigeria to compete in track and field at Asuza Pacific University. When he arrived on campus the football coach saw that Okoya could not only throw a shot-put, but he could run…fast. They put pads on him at APU and he dominated in both college and then professional football. Okoya had a relatively short career in the NFL, but it was impressive. He earned the name, The Nigerian Nightmare, because he ran defenders over.

Okoya grew up playing soccer in Nigeria. Imagine if he would've settled for an AYSO trophy and stopped there.

Think of all the reject athletes that found their niche as musicians. Or the college drop-out who started a business that improves our lives. Or those for whom school was difficult, so they became teachers to help the next generation flourish.

Sometimes you have to fail to find your way.

Unearned trophies can make us entitled and lazy. In order to uncover your genius you might need to lose some games. To develop a right view of yourself, and a healthy self-esteem, you might have to be honest about where you don't belong—and where you do.

Experiment

Questions:

What have you discovered about yourself and your story that makes you unique? How could your uniqueness benefit others?

Actions:

Study this list of tips for building a healthy self-esteem...[7]

1. Recognize that your humanity is common, but that God designed you special and unique, just the way you are.

2. Reject the idea that you are in competition with others. You are simply becoming the best version of you—the person God designed you to be.

3. Recognize that self-worth is innate. Your self-worth has nothing to do with your net-worth. Neither is your self-worth dependent on your performance.

4. Accept 100% accountability for your actions and decisions. There is no one to blame.

5. Appreciate that mistakes are stepping stones to achievement. Mistakes are a prerequisite for future success.

6. Realize that life is a journey to be embraced one day at a time.

7. Recognize that praise pays—even when things aren't going well. Be liberal with encouragement.

We build self-esteem by focusing on what's right, good, and positive. Catch yourself in the act of doing things right. People who feel good about themselves are healthier, happier, and more productive.

---

7. *from my friend Eric Boles*

"Talent is God's gift to you. What you do with it is your gift back."
—Eric Boles

GREATNESS

"Greatness is a choice. It is not about being gifted, or talented, or more fortunate than others. It's about a choice we all can make."
—Robert Kiyosaki

Bronnie Ware is an Australian nurse who spent several years working with dying patients in the final 12 weeks of their lives. She wrote about her patients' near-death epiphanies in a blog called *Inspiration and Chai*.

Ware writes of the clarity of vision that people gain at the end of their lives and what we can learn from their wisdom. "When questioned about any regrets they had or anything they would do differently," she says, "common themes surfaced again and again."

Here is the number one regret of the dying, as witnessed by Ware:

1. I wish I'd had the courage to live a life true to myself, not the life others expected of me.

"This was the most common regret of all. When people realize that their life is almost over and look back clearly on it, it is easy to see how many dreams have gone unfulfilled. Most people had not honored even a half of their dreams and had to die knowing that it was due to choices they had made, or not made." [8]

Authenticity: To know yourself, and live honestly before others.

When I met my friend Marshall he was miserable. He was in college, living in an apartment alone, and pursuing his father's dream for his life. Every time his parents came to visit, Marshall spent $100 on housecleaning for a 700 square foot apartment. He felt that if he didn't go over his bathroom tile with bleach and a toothbrush that his father would find flaws, and flaws represented laziness.

Marshall walked through college with a heavy burden, pushing himself to high-performance levels in his business school courses. It was bad enough that

---

he didn't make it into his father's alma mater. At this point, he'd better be a high-achiever.

High performances is a good thing. But not at the expense of your soul. Marshall confided in me that he often fantasized about buying a sailboat and taking it south...never to see his family or face his pre-determined future in business again.

What happens to a person like Marshall? Eventually, the pressure will get to him. The pressure gets to all of us. It just shows up in different ways. Some drink to excess. So become addicted to porn or sex. Others eat themselves obese.

Our souls long for an authentic life.

* * *

One of most triumphant, heroic, and famous stories from the Hebrew Scriptures is that of David and Goliath. Most people know that David killed the nine-and-half-feet-tall Goliath with a sling shot and a stone. But did you know that David's moment of bravery was almost undermined by his king and other well-meaning soldiers?

You can read 1 Samuel 17 for the precise biblical account, but here's my paraphrase.

The Israelites are cowering behind their shields. The enormous giant has just called them out. If any one of them were willing to face him toe-to-toe, there would be no need for mass bloodshed. The problem was, no one would face the giant.

David showed up during the standoff, bringing supplies to his brothers—the real soldiers. But when David heard about how the giant was taunting Israel's finest, and how not one of the soldiers had the courage to do anything about it, something happened inside of him. Looking back, it was probably an out-of-body experience. But he had a conviction that overrode his caution. Rational arguments of size and strength didn't cross David's mind. He believed in something bigger than the giant. He believed that God was for him.

"I'll fight him," David shouted. It took awhile for people to take him seriously. But soon enough, David was taken in front of the king. The king didn't believe David had a chance in hell, but it was becoming clear that someone needed to do something. Perhaps David could just wear the giant down—tire him out, then other soldiers might attack a lesser enemy.

So the king gave David his shot. Thinking he was doing David a favor, the king insisted that David wear his own royal body armor. Since the king was king and David was a lowly shepherd, David smiled and tried it on. It didn't fit. It made David look like a 12-year-old trying on his dad's clothes. Not-to-mention the fact that the armor was heavy and would've weighed David down. David declined the armor suit. He also refused the kings spear, and sword, and shield… These things were obviously the normal tools for battle, but David wasn't a normal soldier. He was simply a boy with strong convictions.

David walked out toward the giant, told him that the days of dishonoring the people of God were over, and with one whip of his leather slingshot, he sunk a rock between the eyes of the Goliath. Game over.

Had David tried to wear the king's armor, his accuracy would have been thrown off. Had David tried to use the king's sword, his lack of physical strength would have been exposed. But David did what David had done in the fields protecting his sheep. He used the tools and skills that he had developed in the environment in which God had prepared him. David didn't know that God had been preparing him, but He had.

Only you can be you. And there will be a day, a moment, when you're given a new opportunity—a break, a promotion, an invitation—and you'll be faced with pressure from above and below to use the tools of the previous person. You'll be expected to do things a certain way in a certain time. But it's up to you to remember where you come from and the God who created you. He's prepared you. He's gifted you. And only you can be you.

"The first sign of greatness is when a man does not try to act great."
—Dale Carnegie

Greatness is not a destination. It's not a place to which to aspire. And it's not finally getting to wear the king's armor.

Contrary to our culture of how-to's and hall of fames, you will not be great by trying to be great. You accomplish things, earn things, and achieve results. But greatness is about you being you. To be great you must face your giants, stand by your convictions, and be who God designed you to be. Anything else is inauthentic.

Experiment

Question:
What do you believe makes a great life?

Action:
Try on a new habit. Every morning direct your day by filling in the following blanks…

I am: _____
(the main thing to affirm about me today)

I will: _____
(the main focus of my day)

I won't: _____
(the main distraction from my focus today)

"When we see others beginning to live their authentic selves, it drives us crazy if we have not lived out our own."
—Steven Pressfield, The War of Art

WHOLE

"The first wealth is health."
—Ralph Waldo Emerson

The doctor told my friend Chloe that she would no longer be able to have kids. It had been six months since her "womanly cycle" had called it quits. The consequences of excessive workouts, extreme dieting, and emotional stress had taken their toll. Chloe had thought she was disciplined in a commitment to her "health", but it was actually her health she was killing.

Chloe got support at our church. She joined several other women as they talked about their body image, their worth, and what it means to be healthy. With the support of those women and her husband, she began to back off her obsessive behavior. Soon she found herself on a philanthropic trip to the Philippines—getting the focus off herself and serving the poor and malnourished in a developing country. Chloe's heart changed. Her thinking changed. And then, God healed her body.

Chloe and her husband conceived their first child on that very trip in the Philippines.

* * *

There's more to you than meets the eye. You are more than just a body. "Health" means more than skinny, or just not being sick. Fundamentally, health is about the well-being of your whole self—everything that makes up you—including:

- physical attributes
- mental capacities
- emotional engagement
- spiritual connection

All of these things weave together and act as one, making you who you are and giving you your current experience of life as you know it. That's how you were designed.

A common misconception about health is that it's primarily about physical disease, weight, or exercise. It's much more than that. In fact, Webster's Dictionary defines health as "a flourishing condition: well-being."

Are you enjoying a state of well-being? Do you feel like you're flourishing?

Consider all the different parts that make up who you are: physical, mental, emotional, spiritual.

The spiritual connectedness part of you—while invisible—suggests to your consciousness that there is more to life than what you see and touch. It reminds you that you have a Maker who has had your unique design in mind all along. Not only that, but He's given you a reason and a purpose to live.

Your emotional faculties manage your feelings, personal relationships, interactions with others, and with your own self-image. Emotions at their best invigorate and enhance your life. When they are damaged or out of control, they can work to your detriment. That's why emotional self-care is an important part of holistic health.

Your mental capacities make sense of the world around you. Your mind is always engaged—the left brain analyzes and calculates; the right brain senses and reacts. Your body does what your mind tells it to do. Your emotional and spiritual well-being, as well, are very much influenced by what your mind chooses to focus on, and the meaning it assigns to incoming data.

Physical well-being is the most obvious of all because it's visible and tangible—and most people are visually oriented. That's one reason people are so concerned about the health and appearance of their bodies. And, after all, this body is the only one you get. There's no new model or replacement if you're not careful with the one you were given.

Because of the complexity with which humans were designed, the health of our physical bodies will only be sustained by the health of our whole person—by our overall well-being. But most people don't pay attention to their whole selves. Most people over-emphasize one and neglect the others to their detriment. Unfortunately, most of us don't realize we're lacking in an area of our health until it's too late. Like a marathon runner experiencing dehydration on mile 21, it's too late. If she hasn't hydrated enough along the way, she can't make up for it in the final leg of the race. She'll collapse and need an IV—unlikely to finish the race in a manner worthy of her training.

If you don't take care of yourself—your physical, mental, emotional, and spiritual self—you'll drop out of the race. You'll need to be sidelined at some point to receive emergency attention. That's a Significant Life Event...or a tragedy by way of breakdown. These take the forms of divorce, diabetes, depression, DUI's, and other disasters. Don't wait until you're in dyer straights to get healthy. Start now.

Experiment

Questions:
Which if these areas of your life gets the most attention? What gets the least?

Actions:
Circle a healthy habit for each category that you will start this week.

Physical
- Jump on a trampoline for 5 minutes every morning
- Run four days a week
- Eat fresh vegetables with every dinner
- Swim three days a week
- Go for weekly hikes with a friend

Mental
- Read a book for 30 minutes every day
- Watch a Ted Talk (Ted.com) twice a week
- Do a puzzle (sudoku, crossword, etc) every morning
- Discuss local or global issues with a friend every week
- Subscribe to a magazine that interests you

Emotional
- Journal about your feelings at the end beginning or end of each day
- Go to a good counselor every other week for six months

- Talk to a trusted friend about your fears and struggles once a week
- Write down things you're thankful for everyday
- Babysit someone's kids for free once-a-month—and play with the kids

Spiritual
- Volunteer in your community once a week
- Go to church at least three times a month
- Join a small group or a support group
- Read the book of John (fourth gospel in the New Testament)
- Set an alarm on your phone to pray for two minutes everyday at 2pm

BODY BASICS

"Every man is the builder of a temple called his body."
—Henry David Thoreau

There's an older gentleman named James who I know from the gym. At first glance, you wouldn't think of him as an avid exerciser. He's heavy. He wears stabilizing shoes. And his workout apparel is not the latest and greatest from Under Armour or lululemon.

And yet, there he is, at the gym, five days a week, like clockwork.

He's only on the main floor with equipment for about 10 minutes. Then he does this walk-swim motion in the pool before sitting in the sauna. That's his routine, and he's faithful to it.

When asked about his 10-minute lifting sessions, James said, "Well, I know it's not much. But, to tell you the truth, I started at about 10 seconds. So I feel pretty good about where I am today." He made himself laugh. "I really like doing pull-downs (the exercise on a cable where you pull the bar from overhead to your chest). I guess mainly because no part of my body hurts when I do it," he added with another chuckle. ''I just do a couple exercises that I like to do, and I figure I'll add more the stronger I get."

Genius.

James has discovered the World's Greatest Exercise. Do you know what it is?

The World's Greatest Exercise is…the one you'll do!

Seriously.

A lot of people have great intentions for their workouts. They have lofty goals for building their bodies and getting in shape. Or they recall the physical stamina they once had in their youth and use that as their standard. I have a message for that person: Lower the bar!

Here's the ironic thing: When you lower the bar that's preventing you from taking action, you actually raise your standards. Right now, the higher bar—for example, comparing yourself to others or to the college-aged version of you—is preventing you from having any real standard in the present. You might think you have high standards, but it's very likely just a facade that's keeping you from action.

By taking a small step immediately, like James is doing, you break the pattern of being defeated. Whether you're experiencing a workout slump, a rut, apathy, or boredom, you can jump back in and spare yourself the guilt of not being where you think you ought to be. Where you think you should be is an illusion. You are where you are, and you can only start there.

Lower the bar and raise your current standards.

"We cannot do everything at once,
but we can do something at once."
—Calvin Coolidge

* * *

Train and build your body because you appreciate it. Not because you hate it. What good is physical wellness if you're emotionally anorexic? Don't starve your self-image. Appreciate what you have...then maximize it! Make it even healthier.

My friend Jeff appreciates the uniqueness of his body. Jeff has Down syndrome, which can be readily seen in his physical appearance. But Down syndrome is not a downer for Jeff. He is confident in how God made him.

One morning, when Jeff was a teenager, he was upstairs alone in his bathroom and his mother heard him talking to himself. She slowly made her way upstairs to see if he was in need of help. As Jeff's mom approached his slightly-open bathroom door, she saw Jeff standing on top of his bathroom counter in his "tighty-whities" (underwear), triumphantly posing in front of the mirror in all his glory. Not realizing he had company, Jeff stood atop his counter—champion of his bathroom--content with his physical shape. Striking a pose with arms flexed, one leg extended, he said with admiring affection, "Thank you, ThighMaster!"

Jeff appreciated the way God made him. He wasn't looking at the world's definition of a "perfect" body in that mirror. He was looking at reality.

You won't see Jeff on the cover of health magazines or in fragrance commercials. But those things don't matter. They don't even cross Jeff's mind in the first place. Jeff understands something that many people never figure out: *who we are is beautiful.*

What do you think about your body? If you're like most people, you compare your body to some airbrushed "ideal" you've seen in magazines or on TV. Is that helpful motivation?

The fact is, our culture sells discontentment. That's because as long as you and I are discontent, we'll spend more money to try and feel better. So advertisements and media provoke our dissatisfaction with ourselves. The result is that we spend our lives pursuing an impossible ideal—and they make lots of money. Thousands of dollars, surgeries, and tears later, we're still unhappy.

Worse yet, many people live life with the sincere belief that they are less than, sub-par, or unimpressive. And that's not true.

The truth is that God designed you unlike any other human who has ever lived, or will ever live. You are unique, and you are well-made.[9] So, train your body…build your strength…make the most of your physical assets. But start from a place of gratitude and respect for the miracle that is you.

Experiment

Questions:
How do you think popular culture (media, advertising, expectations, etc.) works against your ability to be comfortable with how you look physically? What are some characteristics that you like about yourself?

Action:
Anytime something comes into your mind telling you that you're ugly or not enough, repeat this in your head over and over: "God made me, and God does great work. I am grateful for who I am, and I am a work in progress."

I praise you because you made me in an amazing and wonderful way. What you have done is wonderful…You saw my bones being formed as I took shape in my mother's body. When I was put together there, you saw my body as it was formed. All the days planned for me were written in your book before I was one day old.
—Psalm 139:13-16

9.   *Psalm 139:14*

PREHAB

"Life is but a mass of habits—practical, emotional, and intellectual...systematically organized for our greatness or grief."
—William James

You've heard of rehab—or rehabilitation. It's a place we go when an injury, addiction, or depression digs a hole for us and we need help to get out.

I grew four inches my freshman year of high school. I was a knobby-kneed rail of kid trying to keep my balance in a stiff breeze. Unfortunately, my ligaments didn't keep pace with my bones. Both my shoulders slipped out of my joint in my sophomore basketball season.

I still remember the first time it happened. I was on the basketball court. I got a normal pass from a teammate, but it was slightly behind me. I had to stretch my arms back to catch the ball, and when I did, my left shoulder slipped out of its socket. I dropped the ball and fell to ground. The arm slipped itself back into place, but I was freaked out. Am I falling apart?

I went to an orthopedic specialist and he told me that I needed to ice, rest, and then strengthen the small muscles around my shoulder. I had to rehabilitate the strained shoulder.

Rehab strengthens us after an injury. Prehab strengthens us to prevent injury. Prehab is preventative and progressive. Prehab is about building strength and health so that you don't need rehab.

When you're Prehabbing you're preparing. You're anticipating challenges ahead. You're getting yourself—and keeping yourself—in a posture to maintain health and overcome obstacles.

Prehab leads to sustainability.

I've heard a lot of people say that they would get into shape if they had a goal or event or contract (like a professional athlete) to drive them. I think that's a cop-out. That's like saying you won't put out a kitchen fire because you're not a fireman. Or you won't process your feelings because you're not a psychologist.

Think about healthy habits as Prehab. You have the capacity to build habits into your life to sustain health.

Remember the chapter on Scripting Solutions. You have to clearly define the Prehab progress you want to see. Consider the following basic ideas—taken from other parts of this book:

1. Physically, I want to have more energy, wake up alert, and exercise four days a week.

2. Mentally, I want to identify my negative thoughts and intentionally replace them with empowering truths, morning and night.

3. Emotionally, I want to train myself to forgive quickly and maintain a confident posture in every new situation.

4. Spiritually, I want to pray a prayer of gratitude and look for someone else I can serve every day.

When it comes to setting personal goals going forward, I encourage you to consider all four aspects of who you are. Everyday you're getting more or less healthy: physically, mentally, emotionally, and spiritually. If you wait for an annual checkup and a doctor to tell you that you're eating crap, drinking too much, and have no lung capacity, you're just plain dumb. (But you can change.) This is the only body you get. Your mind is hungry to be engaged. Your heart is desperate for authentic relationships. And your spirit is dry until directed to its Designer.

Experiment

Questions:
What area(s) of your life do tend to neglect? What would it look like to Prehab your life instead of waiting for future injury?

Actions:
Go back and look at your Main Thing and Values. Create a Prehab plan to bring health to your body, mind, heart, and spirit.

BLIND SPOTS

"Anybody can say charming things and try to please and to flatter, but a true friend says unpleasant things...for he knows that then he is doing good."
—Oscar Wilde

I was in the car with a friend recently. We were driving on a city street, but it wasn't overly crowded. We had just been laughing and joking and talking about something funny. Then, there were a few moments of silence. (Silence among friends is good. If there's silence, and neither of you feel awkward, you're probably good friends.)

But the silence was interrupted by chaos. My friend was driving, and decided to change lanes. Because the road seemed empty, he neglected to signal or look over his shoulder. Then came a honk and the sound of swerving tires. My friend jerked the wheel back into his lane and let out a brief and momentary shrill that resembled that of a 12-year-old girl. Realizing that his nervous reaction sounded like a pre-teen in pig-tails, he followed it up with a barrage of locker-room vulgarity, as if to tilt the scale back to masculine. But I wouldn't let him off that easy.

"You realize what just happened, right? A) You just about ran a lady off the road. B) You almost wrecked your car, and maybe our lives. And, C) you screamed like nine-year old Macaulay Culkin." Like I said, we were good friends.

The culprit? Yes, laziness. But also, his blind spot. He had looked in the rearview mirror and seen nothing. He colorfully assured me (or himself) that he had also looked into passenger side mirror and saw that the coast was clear. But it wasn't. There was a spot that the mirrors missed.

Everybody has a blind spot.

It's similar to a smelly house. If you visit someone and their house stinks, you can be sure that they don't know it stinks. If they did, they would spray a bunch of stuff all over and put their animals outside before you came. But the reason they don't know it smells bad is because the scent starts small and increases over time (like the poor frog in the boiling pot, I guess). Sometimes it takes someone else to tell you the truth.

I have a lot of friends, but most of those relationships only get to a certain level. I can make people feel close quickly. But then I have a some barriers to further entry that only a few get beyond.

I think that's okay, as long as we know the truth about ourselves. And as long as we have at least one or two people that have an "all-access" pass to our lives. And that requires discernment. Because some people love to tell you your house stinks. They might be jealous of you for some other reason, so anytime they smell an odor, they make sure to dramatize it and put you in your place.

Others genuinely want to help, but they come across abrasive or demeaning—as if they're better than you. Maybe their blind spots are different than yours. Something that is difficult or nagging for you is simple—a non-issue—for them. Regardless, those people have gotten too comfortable being the "pointer-outer," and probably need their own dose of humiliation.

Still other friends seem super helpful, empathizing and encouraging at first… but you find out later that they're own personal issues have to deal with running their mouths. These friends should wear "proceed with cause" signs. You want to be real with them, but you just shouldn't, because they talk too much.

The key is to find a couple good friends. Friends who can tell you something you hate to hear, but you can trust they love you and truly have your best interest in mind. These are the friends you can trust with your blind spots.

Experiment

Question:
What characteristics do you need to develop to be a "blind-spot friend" to someone else?

Action:
If you're like me, you find it easier not to deal with the confrontation issues of life. But if there's no one in your life that loves you enough—and feels comfortable enough—to expose your blind spots, your house is going to wreak.

Make a call today. Take a risk. Trust a friend.

> *As iron sharpens iron, so one person sharpens another.*
> —Proverbs 27:17

INFLUENCE 20

> *"What we do in life echoes in eternity."*
> —Maximus, Gladiator

Your life has an echo.

Imagine tossing a stone into still water. There is a ripple effect. The size and scope of the ripple is consistent with the size of the initial action—the splash.

A recent study found that the lives of at least 20 people are *directly* influenced by the negative consequences of every alcoholic. She might think her drinking is a private issue, but, in reality, the ripple effect is hurting at least 20 people.

You may or may not have personal experience with this reality, but the principle is relevant to all of us. I'm calling this the *20 Principle*.

The 20 Principle has profound implications for your life. If an alcoholic, attempting to limit the impact of their vice, burdens 20 unique individuals' lives, how much more of an impact could you be having for good? If someone controlled by "spirits" has a shaping, negative influence on 20 others, then you or I, with a different kind of *spirit*, should be able to make a profoundly positive, lasting impact on *at least* 20 people! After all, we *want* to. We want to do good. We desire to leave a legacy. We hope others see us in a positive light, and that they'll remember us when we're gone.

The 20 Principle suggests that your life will have an enduring impact on at least 20 people—perhaps without you fully realizing it. Now, just think what is possible with a little effort! Think of how you can change 20 lives for the better. And why stop at 20?

* * *

My friend Jean almost died last year. He fell out of a boat and the propeller sliced through one of his legs and his chest. The blade cut several of his ribs and punctured his lung. Floating because of a life vest in a pool of his own blood, Jean thought, "So this is what it feels like to die." He said that because of his faith in God, he did not fear death. In that moment, he experienced peace. He was ready.

"It was like an out-of-body experience. I realized that I had matured—I trusted God. I was not afraid to die. I was actually excited to meet my Maker."

But he hasn't. Not yet.

Jean looked up from the water, his body beginning to shut down, and he saw his two kids. In that moment, he prayed, "God, is my work here done? Those kids still need me. Should I fight to live?"

Jean had the sense that God responded to him, saying, "You can fight."

Jean fought for his life and he survived. Laying in the hospital bed he woke up from multiple surgeries with a new outlook.

"I woke up, realized that I was alive, and that I was alive for a purpose. My body was a mess. But my spirit was energized with more passion for living than ever before. I was immediately determined to make my life count."

Jean continued… "After hugging my family and praising the doctors and nurses, I settled back in for some rest. As I closed my eyes I considered all the things I would do, how I would re-prioritize my life, and how I would impact the world. Then, I had an awakening that shocked me. I realized that the sense of purpose and calling I felt in that hospital bed was far more tangible and passionate than ever…but it was not new. I had just as much purpose and significance each day of my life *before* the accident. I just didn't realize it."

Jean's influence has expanded. He looks for opportunities to encourage and inspire others. He's an active and engaged husband and father. He's great at his job and his co-workers love him. Jean's been interviewed and invited to speak different places. He tells me that he tries to make the most of his opportunities—each encounter, every interaction, day after day.

You don't need a near-death experience to realize that God has a plan for your life. You don't need to look up into the face of your crying children to choose to make the most out of today. You can simply choose—choose to believe that your life is significant today.

The bible teaches that *life is God's gift—make the most of it!* [10]

There is something special in you. No one else has your fingerprint. And no one else can leave the imprint on this world that you can leave...that you must leave.

Regardless of your setbacks or your fears and frustrations, God is for you. Choose life, and trust that God will *never leave you or abandon you.* [11]

Don't wait until there's blood in the water. Maybe, for you, this book is a neon sign on your dead-end highway, or a life vest in deep waters. Learn from the lives of others and make the most of the time you've been given.

Your life will speak long after you're gone. What will it say about how you chose to live?

Experiment:

Question:
When is the last time you thought about the imprint you're leaving on the world—the legacy you will leave when you die?

Action:
Make a list of 20 people whose lives you already influence. Now, ask yourself for each person: Are they grateful, indifferent, or regretful for your influence?

10.   *Eccl 5 MSG*

11.   *Deut 31:6*

"'Someday' is a disease that will take your dreams to the grave with you."
—Tim Ferriss

UNTIL DEATH DOES ITS PART

Your Bucket Life

The Making of a Life

"You cannot change your destination overnight, but you can change your direction overnight."
—Jim Rohn

PEACE + PROGRESS

"Many challenges in life are tensions to managed,
not problems to be solved."
—Andy Stanley

For 30 years my identity was tied to progress, achievement, reputation, and the hope of being "great." I became exhausted from the burden being me—and not really knowing who that was.

After a day of intensive counseling, one brilliant therapist got me to visualize what was robbing me of life and preventing me from enjoying the gift of today. "You're obsessed with your potential," she observed. "And what's your potential?"

I didn't know. It was this ambiguous future where I'd be recognized as special and have a sense that I contributed what I was supposed to in this life.

The therapist stood on the other side of the room holding a rope (like you have on-hand when you're a therapist). She tossed the other end of the rope to me. She told me that she was my ambiguous future "potential" and she told me to hold the rope as passionately as I wanted to see my potential realized. I squeezed with white knuckles. She pulled on the rope. She leaned back and pulled until she pulled me up out of my seat—where I had been sitting next to my wife—and toward her across the room. She kept pulling, further and further. Then she dropped the rope and left me alone where I stood.

There I was, holding a rope by myself, ten feet from my wife and from my life. After the metaphorical journey toward my potential, all that I ended up with was myself and empty rope.

Then she went there. She asked my wife, "How does this make you feel."

Hilary began to cry. "This is exactly how I feel all the time. He pulls away from me. He's critical of himself, so he's critical of me. When I reach for him, he acts like I'm holding him back. I feel alone."

It clicked. I got it. I could see her pain and her loneliness. I could see my grasping for something that might not exist. Maybe, in the future, I'm just me—but older and wiser, having done some stuff. Maybe my obsession with my potential is a prison of my own making. Maybe it's actually killing me, and my marriage.

That Significant Learning Moment taught me that if I don't experience peace *today,* I will never experience it. If I can't be grateful for things I have, not obsessing for more, I'll never be satisfied.

"But with contentment comes laziness and apathy," you might argue. "I want to keep my edge and my drive."

I understand. I do, too. And you can. It's a tension of *both*.

On the one hand, I'm satisfied with life. On the other hand, I'm looking to inspire and bring about positive change—in my own life and for others. It's the mysterious paradox at the center of this thing we call life: *Enjoy it, AND improve it.* Respect the world and change the world. Honor people for who they are, and challenge them to go further still.

The two ideas don't need to be mutually exclusive. You can choose to start enjoying and maximizing your life—today—without losing your creative edge for inspiring change. You can be happy and not lazy. You can be ambitious and not obsessive. You can find the miraculous middle. In fact, you must!

If you don't learn to live in the tension of peace + progress, you'll achieve and never have enough. You'll excel and never be satisfied. You'll become but always be lacking.

Here is what I believe to be the secret to a life of happiness: Be grateful.

Be grateful to your God for your life and every blessing. Be grateful for the capacity to grow and become more than you are today.

Peace + Progress. It's possible.

Experiment

Question:
What pulls you from enjoying the present?

Action:
Interview someone in the later stages of their life. Ask them what they obsessed about during their lifetime and if it was worth it.

"Come to me, all you who are weary and burdened, and I will give you rest. Take my yoke upon you and learn from me, for I am gentle and humble in heart, and you will find rest for your souls. For my yoke is easy and my burden is light."
—Jesus, Matthew 11:28-30

YOUR YARD

"Don't go through life, grow through life."
—Eric Butterworth

Kimi (my late mother-in-law) was a master gardener. You can still find her 82-year-old mom, Gma Pat, in her own garden most days. It runs in the family.

So when Kimi died, Hilary was committed to gardening. She uprooted some of her mom's favorites and planted them at our house, creating a small flowerbed along the side of our garage. Hilary took great care of those flowers and herbs. I remember her commenting that she wasn't as good as her mom, and, of course, she wished her mom was there to help. But she kept on. Daily. She watered and made sure the plants were getting the sun they needed. And they became amazing—vibrant, healthy, beautiful.

Neighbors and family members regularly commented on the beautiful flowers. They asked Hilary for gardening tips. Her consistent attentiveness to these special plants made them brilliant.

The circumstance—her mother's death—that led to Hilary's new passion was awful. But the result was that Hilary tapped into something new—and something old.

Something New: Hilary didn't know she had a passion for gardening until she committed to it. Her mother's death led to this new experience of life.

Something Old: Green proves growth. And growth happens where you water.

* * *

You're killing something, right now.

You're killing something and cultivating something all the time. Life, in a sense, is death-management. You're choosing what gets to live and what will die.

Right now, I'm killing my professional volleyball career. (Don't be sad. I began putting it to death 10 years ago.) Today is my day off, and instead of going down to the beach to play or workout, I'm strapping myself to a computer to finish this book. Why? I only have one life, and I have to choose what is most important with the time I've been given. So I choose to write—to put down in words the experiences and insights that I have in hopes that they'll serve you.

How about you? What are you killing right now in exchange for the mental and spiritual growth you're cultivating? What are you prioritizing? What's being left out? Are you cultivating things that need to die, or killing things that you know should be higher priorities?

The matter of life and death is the most obvious in your significant relationships. Consider the lyrical stylings of Big Sean in Justin Bieber's "As Long as You Love Me": *the grass ain't always greener on the other side, it's green where you water it.*

This hip-hop poet sheds light on a true reality: The grass really does seem greener "over there," as opposed to your position of normalcy, routine, and familiarity. But while it seems greener, and has the allure and promise of making you happy, it always disappoints.

Rather, the truth woven into the fabric of nature is this: what you cultivate and care for will grow and flourish. What you don't cultivate and don't care for will slowly die.

Be slow to chase what you don't have. Be quick to water what's already yours.

Experiment

Questions:

Where are you watering? Who gets your best and who pays the price? Are the most important things getting your best efforts?

Action:

Draw a "T" diagram. On the left, at the top, write: "To cultivate." On the right, at the top, write: "To Kill." And fill in below what things in your life belong under which heading.

GRATEFUL

"The way to love anything is to realize that it may be lost."
—G.K. Chesterton

Have you heard the famously unlikely story of Super Bowl-winning quarterback Kurt Warner? Some have called it the most unlikely underdog story in the history of professional football.

After his small-college career, Kurt went undrafted by the NFL. Still hoping to make an NFL team, Kurt went home to Iowa and worked at his local grocery store in Cedar Falls for $5.50 an hour. After being denied by NFL teams, Kurt tried out for a local Arena Football team, the Iowa Barnstormers. Kurt had great success in his two seasons with the Barnstormers, being named 12th out of 20 best Arena Footballs players of all-time.

In 1997, Kurt was invited to tryout with the Chicago Bears, but an spider bite on his throwing elbow (suffered on his honeymoon) prevented him from trying out. A year later, Kurt was signed but the St. Lewis Rams, but shipped off to their European team in Amsterdam. He led the European league in touchdowns and passing yards.

The St. Lewis Rams brought Kurt back to St. Lewis where he spent the 1998 season on the bench as the third string quarterback.

Let's stop here for a moment. At that time, it didn't look good for Kurt. Even though he'd had success in Europe and in the Arena League, he got little respect in the NFL. And he was about to be 28 years old. Very few NFL players remain in the NFL until the age of 28. By pro sport standards, Kurt was an old man. But he was a man who seized every opportunity that he'd been given, kept showing up for work, and kept pushing himself to improve.

During this same time in his life, Kurt not only married, but became a father. When he met his wife, she already had two children from a previous marriage—one had special needs. The story goes that Brenda (who would become Kurt's wife), was about to cancel their second date because she couldn't find a babysitter for the kids. Kurt responded, "I'm taking you ALL out!"

When the couple married, Kurt immediately adapted both children. Since then, the couple has added five more of their own.

Back to the field:

In 1998, Kurt remained the third-string quarterback, seeing almost no playing time.

In 1999, Kurt was promoted to second-string. In a preseason game, starter Trent Green torn his ACL and the unknown Kurt Warner took over. After his first season as an NFL starting quarterback, Kurt had put together one of the best performances in NFL history, throwing for 4,353 yards with 41 touchdown passes and a completion rate of 65.1%. The Rams' high-powered offense, run by offensive coordinator Mike Martz, was nicknamed "The Greatest Show on Turf" and registered the first in a string of three consecutive 500-point seasons, an NFL record.

Kurt Warner's "zero to hero" season was so unexpected that Sports Illustrated featured him on their October 18 cover with the caption "Who Is This Guy?" He was also named the 1999 NFL MVP at the season's end.

In the 1999 NFL playoffs, Warner ultimately led the Rams to a Super Bowl XXXIV victory against the Tennessee Titans. In the game, he threw for two touchdowns and a Super Bowl-record 414 passing yards, including a critical 73-yard touchdown to Isaac Bruce when the game was tied with just over two minutes to play. Warner also set a Super Bowl record by attempting 45 passes without a single interception. For his performance, Warner was awarded the Super Bowl MVP, becoming the seventh player to win both the league MVP and Super Bowl MVP awards in the same year.

Kurt Warner's career would be up-and-down—a mixture of triumphs, injuries, set-backs and trades. But he would enjoy two more Super Bowl appearances, another NFL MVP award, and countless other accolades. Kurt might have been the finest, and most unlikely, superstar of his era.

But in the Arizona town Kurt resides, he's known for much more than throwing the football. Not only does Kurt run his own non-profit called the "First Things First Foundation," but he and his family also have an astonishing habit.

Any time the Warner family goes out to dinner they pause before their meal and pray. They always thank God for His generous blessings in their life, and for how He constantly provides for them. At the end of the meal they practice another habit of gratitude. They subtly look around the restaurant, notice who's sitting nearby, and then take turns deciding what other table's dinner they will buy. Whichever child has the night to choose will select the table, tell dad, and dad (Kurt) slips his card to the server telling him or her to charge the other party's meal to his credit card as well. Then, they're off. No parade. No acknowledgement. No fanfare. Just blessing.

Generosity comes from a grateful heart.

I recognize that you might be inclined to compare yourself, your story, and your resources to Kurt Warner and say, "Sure, but with everything that he has, who wouldn't be grateful and generous!" But know this: There is someone somewhere saying they exact same thing as they compare their life to yours.

> *Then I observed that most people are motivated to*
> *success because they envy their neighbors. But this, too, is*
> *meaningless—like chasing the wind.*
> —Solomon

Envy kills gratitude.

I'm a recovering envier. I'm not "fixed," by the way. I can relapse at any time. But I've identified the problem, and I'm beating envy back like a dirty, diseased dog.

Picture me, in the back of large auditoriums, looking speakers and leaders up and down, comparing myself, criticizing... "That was a weak illustration. He keeps backing away from the front of the platform. He's insecure. He's overly polished and inauthentic. I wonder if he still believes any of this. How old are those pleated pants anyway?"

I'm not proud of it. The reality is that it was *me* who was insecure. I knew I was supposed to be (or at least wanted to be) a leader and communicator, but I didn't know how that would play out, or how good I'd be. So I was critical of others. Already in my young life, I've had to go through a lot of pain and humiliation to break some of these patterns from my mind.

We envy and judge the people and things we most resemble. I don't envy musicians—because I'm not one. But I've envied speakers and leaders because that's what I want to do.

But there's problem with that. When you criticize or compare, you never win. If you compare yourself to someone who is better at something, you will be insecure. If you find that you are better, you'll be prideful. Either way, it's bad for you. Stop comparing.

Instead, cultivate gratitude. You can choose to be sincerely grateful. You can trust that the desires in your heart are there for a reason, and that you'll take steps each day toward your goals...AND still be fundamentally grateful for the life you have RIGHT NOW!

* * *

The Psalmist understood a secret of the universe, writing: *Come into His gates with songs of thanksgiving.*[1]

There is a password for accessing God's presence: "Thanks!"

If you have felt disconnected from God—for 10 minutes or 10 years—do whatever you have to do to get yourself sincerely grateful. God just might show Himself to you.

* * *

The primary antidote for depression is gratitude. In fact, gratitude is the antidote for frustration, pride, comparison, and all forms of selfishness.

My friend Jason thought he was going to be professional football player but didn't get invited to tryout. Depression crept in. He lay in bed for weeks.

Later, he thought he was going to be a football coach at his favorite private school but they didn't get hire him. Depression came back with a vengeance. He was so set on one particular outcome that he struggled finding purpose and promise in the context of whatever each day might bring.

If you're battling depression or purposelessness, start at the start: Be grateful that you're alive. Be thankful that God decided to put air in your lungs. Tell God 'thank you' that you can see or hear these words, and that your mind can process these ideas. Then, tell God that you're grateful for how He made you. Even if it's a stretch today, list things that you appreciate about how He designed you—your body, your sense of humor, your ability with people or projects, your capacity to figure things out or put

---

1. *Psalm 100:4*

things together…Anything you can think of, thank God for it. *Every good gift comes from Him.*[2] Feelings follow action. Start practicing gratitude.

Experiment

Question:

What are you doing out of gratitude for the life you've been given? If you're not grateful for your life, what lies are stealing your passion?

Action:

Try a gratitude habit. Start by listing the things you're grateful for. Then do something about it—something generous. You might not have enough money to buy someone's meal at a restaurant, but you can do something.

Give thanks to the Lord, for he is good; his love endures forever.
—1 Chronicles 16:34

I WOKE UP

"When you arise in the morning, think of what a precious privilege it is to be alive—to breathe, to think, to enjoy, to love."
—Marcus Aurelius

My wife, Hilary, wakes up happy most of the time. It's part of her child-like nature that inspires me. Whether it's in the morning or from a nap—it doesn't matter—she'll greet the world once again, "I woke up!"

I might still be asleep, or reading, or watching television. But it makes me smile when I hear the gentle but cheerful, "I woke up!" An announcement. I'm awake. Pay attention. I'm here. And I thought you should know.

What if every morning was like coming out the womb and into existence again? But less messy and awkward.

"Whoa… I'm awake. This is cool…

"So…I'm alive. Life didn't discontinue while I slept. Time marches on. And it's a brand new day. Thanks, God.

Everyday is a new start. And everyday can be a new adventure—if we simply adapt that attitude.

---

2. *James 1:17*

Maybe it partly depends on how you wake up. In the "Action" element below, I'm going to invite you try something new this week. Keep a journal or notebook or note card next to your bed. As soon as you wake up, write down the thoughts that are filling your mind. Do you wake up hopeful and excited? Are you grateful for the gift of another day? Or is your experience more typical of Americans: overwhelmed, anxious, bored? Write down your feelings. Think about your thoughts. What's happening underneath what's happening?

As you're getting ready for work, or for your day, consider why you woke up feeling like you did. What have you been trained to believe about life that even the moment you wake up, those ideas flood your perception of this new day?

Here are some thoughts and feelings that I've had:

- I slept until 7am—I'm already behind
- Why did I watch that stupid show last night?
- What's on the calendar for today?
- I don't feel like working out
- I need better clothes
- I could stand to lose five pounds

Granted, these thoughts are not overly critical or depressing. One might even suggest that they're "fine" or "normal." But I want a *new normal.* I want to wake up with passion and energy and enthusiasm. I want to wake up excited, grateful, joyful, expectant.

I know this is possible because I've done it before, and those are great days. But it takes a mind-shift: from focusing on what's wrong—or could go wrong—to focusing on the good—and what could be.

We've talked about that in a previous chapter—you'll see what you look for—and you'll feel the way you think. Today is the day to begin to wake up with this new outlook.

For much of my life I woke up feeling behind, like I wasn't far enough along. I was critical of people close to me because I thought that they must be holding me back. I compared myself to others and didn't enjoy my life. That was until Kimi died.

When my mother-in-law died something happened to me. We were living in her home so Hilary could care for her around the clock. I watched Hilary wake up early everyday, refusing to waste time crying, jump out of bed, and go downstairs to make the most of the day with her mama.

Kimi didn't want to travel. She didn't want to shop. She didn't wish had been more successful. She didn't regret not being rich or famous. She simply woke up, prayed to God for a pain-free day, and spent time with her family.

The family didn't know there would only be 80 days. But we made the most of them. We told stories, played cards, watched movies, and laughed at everything funny. Her family made sure that Kimi felt loved—right down to the morning when Kimi didn't wake up.

Each day you wake up is a special day. Even if there's no terminal diagnosis, there are people you can cherish today. There is passion you can embrace.

You can choose to appreciate the things and people that matter.

You can choose child-like joy.

"Joy does not simply happen to us.
We have to choose joy and keep choosing it every day."
—Henri Nouwen

Experiment

Question:

How would a joyful and hopeful mindset make today a better day?

Action:

Practice thanking God for being alive, right now. And let that be a new habit— the first thing you do every morning. Keep a journal beside your bed this week to take note of what you wake up thinking and feeling. Create a new normal. Improve your life by appreciating it.

THE DAILY DRIP

"Men's natures are alike; it is their habits that separate them."
—Confucius

When I think of a "drip," three things come to mind:
1.   Rumors of old Chinese torture
2.   Coffee in the morning
3.   An IV in my arm

My parents are coffee junkies. I never understood the appeal. It's black, it doesn't taste good, and it's addicting. I'll pass. But clearly I'm in the minority, so I don't want to disrespect the bean.

Yet I do want to call attention to the fact that a large percentage of humans can't motivate themselves to get on with their day without their morning fix. Yo Joe!

Then, take an IV, for example. Hopefully you've never been sick enough to need one. The IV needle goes into a patient's vein, usually in the forearm. The bag contains the fluid and it hangs near by, dripping the appropriate amount of liquid nutrients the body requires. The IV drip literally keeps people alive, and revives individuals who are dehydrated or who aren't receiving the necessary nutrients naturally.

I know of a professional athlete who was recently competing in spite of having flu symptoms. He was so sick and dehydrated that he had to receive an IV during halftime of the game, and directly after the game. Apparently you can find the nutrient-drip in locker rooms nationwide.

Let's stretch the metaphor… Do you know your daily drip? What do you need, physically or emotionally, to get you over the hump?

Everyone seems to develop some coping habits to deal with the "daily grind." For some it's coffee every morning. For others it's television…a night-cap…some kind of sexual release, social media, a workout, the great food escape, or spending money.

Do you ever find yourself drawn to any of the above (and there are countless others) like a zombie? None of them are necessarily bad…until they are. Until we can't function without them.

> *"Habit, if not resisted, soon becomes necessity."*
> —St. Augustine

I've found that there are two kinds of daily drips: *natural* and *supernatural*. I listed several of the natural coping mechanism above. The natural suggests that I'm on my own and need to learn to deal with life as I know it. Therefore, I develop "outlets" to give me a break from carrying the weight of the world. Our outlets are rooted in discontentment with the realities of life we've come to know and expect.

Supernatural drips are entirely different. A supernatural drip reminds me that I'm not in control; that there is an Architect of the universe that I can trust. And His creation goes beyond my natural experience in the world.

To connect with the supernatural is to connect with God. To connect with God is to stay hydrated, spiritually. To trouble-shoot our way through life with natural coping habits is a road to frustration and dysfunction.

I'm not going to write you a prescription for sustained spiritual hydration. We can connect and sustain in different ways. But I have no hesitation in telling you that you need a spiritual IV of some kind.

Our world is material and physical, and material things lobby for all our attention and focus. But we are spiritual beings.

C.S. Lewis said, "You don't have a soul. You are a Soul. You have a body."

How are you caring for your soul? Here are a few ideas:

- Take a walk every morning, and as you notice the creation, consider its Creator.
- Host people in your home on regular basis, and talk about spiritual things. (You might want to start by reading this book together. Spiritual conversations can be awkward until the group has some kind of baseline.)
- Memorize a short verse from Scripture everyday (or weekly).
- Say a short prayer for everyone you come in contact with under your breath.

Experiment

Question:

What's your sustaining spiritual drip?

Action:

Choose one of the ideas above or something else that will work for you. Commit to a daily spiritual habit for the week.

THE HABIT THAT KILLS BAD HABITS

"Eyes that do not cry, do not see."
—Swedish Proverb

Let's say that there are 100 people who want to write a book. They're confident in the Twitter skills, and some even have an active blog, read by at least their mom. If 100 people want to write a book (whether they should or not), only 10 ever will. And of those 10 only 5 will actually get to the point of publishing the content—even in a digital format. And of those 5, only one person will have put in the time, effort, training, and marketing to make any money from the book. One hundred people want to write books. Only 10 actually do it. Only one excels. Why?

It's not about the content. It's not about luck. It's not even about talent. It's about habits. The quality of your productivity is linked to the habits that make up your life.

There is a billion dollar industry devoted to helping you be more productive, set better goals, practice better habits, discipline your demons, etc. You can reduce most of these messages down to three solid and simple principles:

1. List your objectives
2. Prioritize your actions
3. Tackle the most important things first

These are good ideas. You and I would agree that this list makes sense and we should do these things. But we struggle. Even today, as I've set aside an entire day to work on this book, I've allowed myself to be distracted by the following:

- Facebook
- Text messages
- Going for a run
- Watching a bad-lip-syncing video
- Looking online at local real estate listings

The only thing on that list that could qualify as a high priority today is going for a run. The rest of these things were impulsive distractions that took me away from my primary objective. And I write about this stuff!

In his book, *The Power of Habit*, Charles Duhigg describes what he calls the "habit loop." Something takes place around us that triggers our desire for a "reward." We are then compelled to take the actions that our mind thinks will get us that reward.

The reward can be a burst of adrenaline, a thrill, or a brief connection with another person. The reward can also be the avoidance of a negative outcome, like when we distract ourselves to avoid feelings or thoughts that we associate with pain or fear.

When we are unaware of our trigger(s) and the reward we pursue, we literally have no choice but to follow the pattern, the habit loop. The result is always disappointing—hence: bad habit. The reward has diminishing returns. Like a drug addict needing a stronger and stronger hit to get the former high. And every time we give way to the loop, we dig the habit groove deeper into our nervous system's hard wiring.

You and I know what is to try and override that habit loop, which is another way of saying "New Years Resolution." But as studies have shown, willpower goes only so far. It's a muscle that tires quickly—much more quickly than the death of the habit we want to be rid of.

In other words, in the battle between immediate and delayed gratification, immediate always wins.

So what do we do?

In an article for Fast Company, Howard Jacobson tapped into a truth that I call *the habit that kills bad habits*.

"Virtually all the strategies of the get-it-done industry consist of some form of time manipulation. Meaning, some way to trick ourselves into doing what, in that moment, we really don't want to do.

Trying to build new habits on top of dysfunctional old ones works about as well as putting a new car body on top of a rusty old engine. If we don't deal with the fundamental issue, no amount of time blocking or beepers beeping or context-based task lists will overcome the pull of the habit mind." [3]

So, you could post sticky notes reminding yourself to focus on your project and not check your phone, email, or social media. And it might work, for a little while. But something will inevitably trigger the habit loop and you'll fall victim to immediate gratification. That is, until you address the fundamental issue.

What's the issue? I don't know what your issue is, but I can give you mine. In my desire for greatness, I sit down to write and I turn the genius knob…but nothing comes out. Internally, subconsciously, I panic. And I want to escape. Enter my habit loop. My subconscious mind wants to distract myself from feeling the feelings that I might not live up to expectations—I might fail; I might fall behind; I might not be who I want to be. Then, I escape. And I regret it. I waste time, I make compromises, I look for cheap thrills to make me feel better—for a few moments.

Escape is the enemy. Your hope is to feel your feelings.

"You've been down there, Neo.
You already know that road. You know exactly where it ends.
And I know that's not where you want to be."
—Trinity, The Matrix

Your next step: Sit in your unwanted feelings and resist the escape.

Feel your feelings, and don't fear them. They don't own you. They are telling you something—something that needs healing, a belief that needs replacing. Maybe your mind needs new data to replace old bad information.

Think about your thoughts.

Speak the truth to yourself.

Resist your escape patterns.

And feel your feelings. It's time to mine up the source of your bad habits. It's not about will-power. It's about dealing honestly with the things you feel under the surface.

Feeling is your road to healing.

---

3.   *How To Develop Strong Time-Management Habits, Even If You've Failed In The Past, by Howard Jacobson, January 25, 2013, Fast Company*

Experiment

Question:
What are the triggers that send you into your habit loop spiral?

Action:
Notice the next time you are triggered. Instead of acting on your usual impulse, sit quietly. Close your eyes. Ask God to help you understand what you're feeling and why your subconscious wants to escape. Write down the lie behind the negative feeling.

Search me, God, and know my heart; test me and know my anxious thoughts. See if there is any offensive way in me, and lead me in the way everlasting.
—Psalm 139:23-24

SCRIPTING SOLUTIONS

"Progress is a nice word. But change is its motivator and change has its enemies."
—Robert Kennedy

Did you know that the offensive coach almost always scripts the first 10 to 15 plays of any professional football game? Before the offense ever sets foot on the field, before they look across at the defense, and before they even determine where their starting position will be, they have scripted their first moves. The scripted plays are based on what the teams know about their opponents and what they know about themselves. If a team has a young quarterback and wants to ease him into the game to let him get comfortable before having to make a big play, the offensive coach will script run plays to start the game. If the coach has great confidence in the quarterback and wants to shock the defense and jump out to a fast lead, he'll likely script them to start throwing the ball aggressively. Either way, these kinds of decisions are made in practice well before the game starts.

In their book, *Switch*, Dan and Chip Heath talk about learning to "script" specific changes you want to see in your life, organization, or community. They argue that it's not enough to make vague, blanket statements about changes you hope to see. "I want to eat healthier," is not clear enough to create change. There's wiggle room, space for the rationalizer in all of us. Instead, more appropriate scripting would be "No more white flour, no more whole milk, and no eating past 8:00 p.m."

My brother Josh went to several doctors about some digestive trouble he was having. One doctor just gave him a pill and said he'd likely deal with this issue the rest of his life—basically said, "medicate, and good luck." Josh wasn't satisfied, so he got another opinion. The new doctor did some preliminary examinations and then gave Josh a major challenge. "I think you're allergic to dairy and gluten. If you want to be sure, and if you want your stomach to heal, you need to completely cut all flours, grains, and dairy products from your diet."

Tough decision. Limit your diet to 30% of the grocery store, or continue with a lifestyle of digestive pain. But the decision was clear—it was black and white. There was no guesswork. Josh took the challenge, and he's a more fit, healthy, and happy man for it.

* * *

The Hebrew culture has historically viewed their word for "learn" differently than we do in English. For an ancient Jewish person, to *learn*, is to understand by putting into practice.

In our information age, we think we "know" a lot. We read books, blogs, Tweets, articles, updates…but we do little about anything. It's not true knowledge. It's the illusion of knowledge.

In fact, many of us feel paralyzed by the excess of information. We're overloaded and not clear about what to do about what we supposedly know.

Take a page out of the Jewish understanding—and take action.

It's been said that you don't master a subject until you teach it. Why? Because you can't explain something you don't yourself grasp. The next level of learning is practice. When insight meets inspiration it leads to action. That's when you truly understand. That's when you truly improve.

It's the same with religious people who fill their mind with theology and ideology but do nothing for others.

As the body without the spirit is dead,
also faith without actions is dead.
—Endnote: James 2:26

Script the shift you want to see. Do you want to start the day differently to-morrow? Do you want to retrain your thoughts and emotions? Write tomorrow's script today.

Scripting will take you from a person with information and good intention to a person of initiation and influence. You can't influence others to make progress if you can't first influence yourself.

Keep the scripts and the shifts *simple*. The most important things in life are simple. They aren't easy, but they are simple.

Experiment

Question:
Is there an area in your life where you would like to see progress, but you haven't yet been clear about what "success" would look like?

Action:
Write down the specific path/plan for the change you want to see. Call and talk to some who's done it if you need help with the plan.

Simple example:
Problem: *I'm not drinking enough water.*
Scripting the Solution: *I'm going to keep a glass on my desk all day. When it's empty, I get up and fill it.*

THINKING ABOUT THINKING

"Men are not prisoners of fate, but prisoners of their own minds."
—Franklin D. Roosevelt

Yoda instructed the young Skywalker, "You must unlearn what you have learned." And you, too, have things in your mind that are holding you back from a new and better experience of life.

In the absence of new truth, your mind will cling to the information already present. It's time to think about our thinking. **It's time for a mental detox.**

You need a mental detox because we live in a society that feeds us a lot of mixed messages and half-truths. Your family of origin was confusing enough. Since those younger years, the world around you been nothing but a barrage of mixed-messages. Should she be a size "0" or an athlete? Should he be at home more or make millions of dollars? Should she have a career or just bigger breasts? Should he drive a nicer car or just be a nicer guy?

Culture tells us so many things about how we should live, look, and behave. Subtly, and often subconsciously, our minds conform to the ways of the world around us. You might be thinking thoughts and believing ideas that you don't even realize you're believing...and you might have no clue why you believe them.

In fact, you might be relying on thoughts and information that are now totally irrelevant—even restrictive—to your growth. The Apostle Paul taught us, *When I was a child, I spoke and thought and reasoned as a child. But when I grew up, I put away childish things.*[4w]

When an elephant is young, the trainer will tie it down with rope and stake. Imagine a leash, preventing the elephant from roaming. The young, small elephant tries to pull out the stake but fails. He stops trying. As the elephant grows he continues to allow himself to be bound by the, now, insignificant little stake in the ground.

You're stronger than you think. There's more in you than you realize. You don't tap into the strength you have everyday, but it's there. You have the strength to change, the power to become, and the courage to move. Things that have held you down in the past don't need to anymore.

---

4.   *1 Cor 13:11*

But you might have a problem. And your problem might be in your mind. The reality is that your sub-conscience mind runs your life, and you might not realize where it's taking you.

If you want to make changes in your life—and you can—it all starts in the mind. And if you want to achieve new or different results it's time for a new strategy and a new way of thinking.

Before you can establish and start living out the new healthy patterns you desire, you have to honestly identify the old ways of thinking (and following) that were getting you nowhere.

Take a few minutes to think long and hard, and examine your perspectives. Think of a conflict, dilemma, or doubt you're facing and write down your beliefs about the issue. Are you beliefs empowering you or tying you down? Are your thought-patterns restricting you or reminding you how strong you are?

Here's an example from my life this week: My wife has been told since she was young that she is "too sensitive." Parents, relatives, coaches, and managers a like have mentioned to Hilary that she should not be so sensitive, or not get her feeling hurt—usually such a comment was in self-defense of something else said or done in poor taste. So, Hilary grew up wondering if she was "crazy." Maybe something is wrong with her. Thankfully, Hilary had an awakening experience this week. After being affirmed by several people over the course of a few days for the manner in which Hilary could listen, relate, and encourage others, Hilary began to see and believe that her sensitivity was a God-given *gift*. Few souls are as honest, transparent, and relatable as Hilary. She makes others feel known and at ease. And she sees it now. She's retraining her brain to believe it. What she was believed was a liability has been an incredible asset all along.

Experiment

Question:
What are some things that are disappointing you, confusing you, or causing you anxiety? How might you need to think differently about those things?

Action:
Consider these key elements of life below. Use the ideas and principles you read about in this book to steer your "Re-thinking" column.

Life Issue	Past Thinking	Re-Thinking
Body Image		
Money		
Career		
God		
Friends		
Family		
Time/Energy		

"You will never outgrow the limitations you place on yourself.
They can only be raised or lowered."
—Bob Moawad

Do not conform any longer to the pattern of this world, but
be transformed by the renewing of your mind. Then you will
be able to test and approve what God's will is—his good,
pleasing and perfect will.
—Romans 12:2

A FUTURE-SHAPING MIND

"A man is but the product of his thoughts.
What he thinks, he becomes."
—Gandhi

Law of Cognition: You become what you most regularly think about.

I remember the marketing campaign of a food brand years ago: "You are what you eat, so you'd better eat right."

I was a kid when I heard it, so it was a strange idea. I knew they couldn't mean that I was literally what I ate, but I wasn't sure of the point. It started to come together for me as a college athlete. Try an intense three-hour practice with a stomach full of pizza. How about running five miles after weight-lifting on a day when all you've eaten are care-package cookies and a glass of milk?

Food is fuel. Food keeps our bodies functioning, performing and reaching their potential.

This same concept applies to our minds. My mom used to say, "Garbage in, garbage out." What we put into our minds will eventually come out through our behavior.

> *"If you wish to know the mind of a man, listen to his words."*
> —Chinese Proverb

Have you heard of the idea of being "brain-washed?" Conspiracy theories have suggested (some have proven) that institutions and individuals have so tampered with the human psyche that victims have completely replaced former ways of thinking and relating to the world with new, usually warped, ways of thinking. They do it by taking them out of the previous environment, completely controlling their new environment, and deconstructing old assumptions with new realities that can't be disproven in the new setting.

Law of Exposure: You think about that which you are regularly exposed.

What do you knowingly expose yourself to on a daily basis? I'm not just talking about negative things – but anything.
- What kind of news do you watch?
- What TV stations?
- What kind of people surround you?
- What music rings in your ears?
- What phone calls do you take?
- What books and magazines do you read?
- What social networks do you trust?
- What websites do you visit?

Do you stop to think that they all have an agenda? And they might be conforming you into their image. You might be willingly following an unknown leader.

How about the exposures you don't even recognize daily? Some have estimated that we subconsciously receive over 3000 branding advertisements everyday. What are they telling you? They are telling you to buy this, change that, become something else, you need more, you should weigh less, you deserve better… and their product will help.

How do we strengthen ourselves against a world of promotion that tries to wash our minds?

I'm usually not a big fan of acrostics—because they are cheesy—but I impressed myself with this one and I think it could actually help:

M – minimize media (control the advertising onslaught)
I – initiate with influencers (seek out the people you want to influence you)
N – notice the noise (learn to recognize and filter out nonsense)
D – detox deliberately (regularly disconnect and refocus on what is true)

If thinking like this helpful, great! If not, use your mind and come up with your own pattern for controlling your thoughts. Remember, if you're not controlling your thoughts, someone else is. The famous Apostle Paul said:... *we take captive every thought to make it obedient to Christ.*[5]

He's talking about controlling our thoughts, making sure we think about things that are true and helpful.

Fix your thoughts on what is true, and honorable, and right, and pure, and lovely, and admirable. Think about things that are excellent and worthy of praise. Keep putting into practice all you learned... Then the God of peace will be with you.[6]

There is a correlation between controlling our thoughts and receiving God's peace. Could you use some peace right now? When I let my thoughts run wild, they go the directions of worry, doubt, fear, and lust. All of which rob me of peace, contentment, and joy.

Control your thoughts today. Direct them toward good. Enjoy God's peace.

Control your thoughts again tomorrow, shape your future.

Experiment

Question:
What are your mind's top three inputs? (I.E.: reality television, radio, magazines)

Action:
Decide how you will filter at least some of what enters you mind today.

A wise person is hungry for truth, while the fool feeds on trash.
—Proverbs 15:14

---

5.   *2 Corinthians 10:5*

6.   *Philippians 4:8-9*

BODY LANGUAGE

Fake it 'til you feel it.

When I was 24, I taught on the stage of one of the largest and fastest-growing churches in America. I sweat through two shirts and might have peed a little bit.

There were 1,500 hundred people in the crowd. (It was their smallest service.) Up until that point, I had only talked for five minutes in front of about 1,000 people at my grandfather's funeral. I took my mind back to that day…my grandfather's casket in front of me. I remember choking up and being nervous, but I think it went well. I helped people to laugh in the midst of our grief. I shared heart-felt sediments. I honored both my grandparents. I did it. I can speak in front of large crowds. I'd done it before, I could do it again.

I told myself, "I belong here. The pastor asked me to do this. So, obviously, he thinks I can pull it off. He sees something in me. I belong here."

Confidence is the conviction that you belong.

My first practice with the Men's Volleyball Team at the University of Southern California I felt like a small fish in a large pond. We lined up on the baseline and I realized I was the second smallest guy on the team. But I felt even smaller. I assumed that my teammates were questioning my ability and wondering why the coach wasted a spot on me.

"What am I doing here?" I talked to my dad later that night. He could tell I was intimidated and unsure of myself. After all, I wasn't groomed for volleyball on the beaches of LA and Orange County like most of my teammates. And the guy starting in front of me was an Albanian, three years and 30 pounds of raw muscle ahead of me.

"You belong there," dad said. "You're great at volleyball already. And you'll work harder than anyone else."

Those same teammates that scared me sweat-less voted me captain of the team the very next year.

There was another guy on the team named Tony, who successfully "faked it till he made it." He talked a lot of nonsense. At first, I didn't like him, but I grew to love him. He hadn't played volleyball as long as the other guys, either. It didn't hurt that he was 6'8", but he still felt behind. So he over-compensated with attitude, talk, and swagger. Where I was more the quite-confident, hard-working type, Tony was over-the-top.

Today, Tony is about to sell his start-up company for a lot of money. He learned to talk himself into confidence and performance. He worked hard, and now it's real—he's living it, and he feels genuine confidence.

* * *

Amy Cuddy, of the Harvard Business School, has done research on the idea of confidence and body language. "We're fascinated with body language," she says. We dissect and analyze and judge people, and in particular we scrutinize public leaders. We make judgments based on body language: whether you're hired for a job, whether you're asked out on a date, whether you get the bid for the job. But, says Cuddy, there is another half that we ignore, another audience. Ourselves. Our body language impacts how we think and feel about ourselves.

You are influencing your own opinion of you by how you carry yourself.

Isn't that backwards? Doesn't my confidence—or lack thereof—dictate how I carry myself? Yes. But I have good news. It can go both ways!

Do an audit of your body. How are you sitting right now? Are your arms crossed? Are you hunched over, smaller, disappearing... Or are you upright, bigger, and taking up space?

Your posture, or body language, is telling you something about how you're feeling. When we shrink ourselves up to take less space, we're feeling insecure. But think of people who take dominant postures—standing tall, spreading out, puffing up their chest... These people exude confidence. Even in the animal kingdom we see this play out.

I did a gorilla-trekking tour in the Congo. A woman on our tour walked between a silverback gorilla momma and her baby. Not good. I saw, live and in person, what was characterized on cartoons growing up: an 800-pound gorilla stood up tall, stomped her foot, pounded her chest, then charged. The woman—just yards from me—tried to jump out of the way, but not before taking a forearm shiver to the side, sending her into the air. Scary. There was no doubt what the gorilla was communicating: I will destroy you if you mess with my baby. Gorilla body language.

Cuddy's research found that you can increase your level of confidence by changing your physical state. In fact, just changing your posture for two minutes can change your confidence level. Hormones are released in your body that "pump you up" and cause you to begin to feel differently. Positive or more confident feelings lead to better performance, which over time can create an ingrained sense of belief about yourself.

A simple example is this: When you are happy, you smile. But if you put a pen sideways in your mouth, between your teeth (forcing your cheeks to raise in a smile), you'll feel more happy. It's science.

Or consider athletes you've seen. Football players especially have intense, testosterone-boosting rituals in the locker room and in the tunnel before coming out to play (I'm picturing Ray Lewis right now). They aren't (completely) crazy. They are onto something. Your body influences your beliefs. If you get yourself feeling powerful, strong, and motivated, you can become so.

When studying her MBA students at Harvard, Cuddy discovered that the posture a student took in class usually determined their level of participation, which usually determined their grade and level of success in the classroom.

She took an interest in one particular student. This student came to her and said that she didn't belong at Harvard. She didn't feel smart enough. She was insecure and nervous to participate in class.

"No," Cuddy told her. (I paraphrase.) "You *do* belong here. You'll make it here. You just need to convince yourself. You need to fake it until you believe it!" She then told her to go home and prepare for class the following day. But on this day, she would sit near the front, sit up straight, look people in the eye, and jump into the discussion whenever she had a window. Even if she felt like she was forcing it or trying too hard. The girl did just that, and, according to Cuddy, she faked it until she believed it. And she made it at Harvard.

Decide you belong. Go gorilla.

You can shape a better future just by standing up straight.

Experiment

Questions:
What does how you're carrying yourself communicate? The way you stand, the way you sit, the manner in which you respond… What are you saying without saying it?

Action:
Practice postures of confidence. Stand up straight. Pick up your head. Pound your chest. Energize your belief in who God's made you to be. Tell yourself you belong here.

eMOTION

"Drink because you are happy,
but never because you are miserable."
—G.K. Chesterton, Heretics

How are your emotions these days? Do you know?

I used to think that being mellow, rarely crying, controlled laughing, and not being very excitable was just normal and fine for me. It was all I knew as an adolescent and young adult. I was controlled, calculated... cool. I was also emotionally detached. And I didn't break until I was broken. And when the dam broke, it really broke. Today, I cry with regularity.

We're all emotional. Some of us hide our emotion; others numb; others let their lives be run by their emotions—letting feelings determine decisions and relationships. But our emotions are one of God's greatest gifts. They are indicators. And they can be a source of power and strength. Emotions give fuel to our lives.

I cried today when I was speaking to a large crowd. (That would never have happened ten years ago.) I didn't anticipate crying. But when I spoke of someone who was serving others in a simple but profound way, emotion rushed over me. My emotion brought emotional intensity to the room. Everyone leaned in and paid extra attention to what I was saying. There is power in emotion.

Some you know the negative side of that power. Maybe a parent leveraged anger or guilt to get a desired response out of you. Maybe your emotions have been manipulated by someone else. Or maybe you have battled your share of broken hearts or days of depression. If so, you know what it's like when negative emotion weighs you down like a wet blanket. You feel like you can't go on, or at least not yet. You wonder if what you feel will ever change.

Here's the truth: God intended your emotions for your health—to bring you life, not death. And you can take action against negative emotions.

Motion changes emotion.

If you find yourself stuck, emotionally, don't settle for that. Change it. Start by getting moving. It might sound simple, but if you can force yourself to get up and move, you're on your way to better feelings. Feeling follow actions. That's why I don't let people tell me that there's nothing they can do about how bad they feel. It's not true. You can move. You can stand up straight. You can run. You can workout. You can kneel and pray. You can make a phone call. You can set a new path by taking one step in the right direction.

Do depressed people stay in bed all day, or are people that stay in bed all day depressed? I've never met a depressed person who was actively and aggressively pursuing life.

Don't complain that you're "not feeling it." Jump to your feet. Move! Feelings will come later.

Experiment

Question:

In what way have you let your emotions run your life? How could you take control of your life and inform your emotions by getting yourself moving in the right direction?

Action:

Tell your closest friend to never let you sit around complaining about not feeling well. Invite yourself to a party, to a sporting contest, or to an activity that will give you a boost and get you moving.

WORDS

My dear brothers and sisters, take note of this:
Everyone should be quick to listen, slow to speak...
—James 1:19

When I was a kid, my parents *made* me listen. They might even go so far as to grab my face and turn it toward them to ensure I was paying attention. Coaches can still get away with that in the heat of a game situation, but it'd be awkward to try it tomorrow at Starbucks or the office. People have to choose to listen to you.

And you have to choose to listen to others. It's not easy. If you're anything like me, your default is distraction. We have the shortest attention spans in history, thanks to our multi-media culture. (Go ahead and tweet that. #ironic) Plus, by nature, we're self-centered. So, halfway through a person's first sentence, I'm already thinking about what I have to do next.

Listening takes discipline. But listening is one of the most appreciated skills you can learn. Perhaps the most honoring thing you can do for someone else is to truly, genuinely listen.

I try to call my Grandma Billie on a semi-regular basis. Grandpa died ten years ago, and she's been adjusting to life on her own ever since. I can't imagine what it's like to suddenly lose your life-partner of 50+ years. But do know this: my Grandma loves it when I call. When I say, "Hi Grandma, it's Caleb!" Her voice perks up with excitement and she'll talk as long as I'll listen. When we finish, she always tells me that my call made her day. And I think she's being sincere.

There's another reason James (in the verse above)[7] is adamant about listening: *it slows down your speaking.*

Slowing down and being more intentional about your speaking is one of the wisest things you can do. It will literally change your life for the better—and quickly. The reason is simple: your words are more powerful than you ever imagined!

Even fools are thought wise when they keep silent; with their mouths shut, they seem intelligent.[8]

Abraham Lincoln is credited with saying: "Better to keep your mouth closed and let people think you're a fool than to open your mouth and remove all doubt." I'm sure you've been around people that run their mouths constantly. Whether they know what they're saying or not, they just keeping saying stuff. And they are obnoxious. (Like the girl you wish you hadn't started a conversation with at a party.)

Words were not meant for your own enjoyment. Words are meant for the edification of others. Words are meant for connection, for encouragement, and for building others up.

An over-simplification, you ask? Nope. Think about the intention of all types conversations. If you are explaining, informing, coaching, clarifying, educating, joking, strategizing, teaching, empowering, or inspiring, the intent is to connect and encourage. Conversations go badly when they shift to demanding, criticizing, condemning, belittling, complaining, attacking, or instigating. No one likes being on the receiving end of those dialogues.

The great communicators are not those who are the most poetic or even articulate. Great communicators are those who are the most intentional with their words. They understand that their words have the power to build up or break down. In fact, words—your words—have the power of life and death.

The tongue can bring death or life;
those who love to talk will reap the consequences.
—Proverbs 18:21 (NLT)

There were two men in the same hospital room. This was a "final stop" kind of hospital room. Both the men where in their final weeks, through they didn't talk about it.

There was a window on one side of the room, right next to the bed of one of the men. The other gentleman was in bed about eight feet away, close to the

---

7. *James was the half-brother of Jesus*

8. *Proverbs 17:28*

door. After a few days of introductions and pleasantries, the man further away from the window asked his new friend what it looked like outside.

"Oh," the By-the-widow-man exclaimed. "It's a beautiful day!"

"In February," By-the-door-man curiously responded?

"Yes, just beautiful." By-the-window-man went on to tell his friend in great detail how beautiful the day was. And then, every day that followed, By-the-window-man would describe to his bed-bounded friend what he saw outside his window. Everything from children playing, to flowers, to rainbows and cloud shapes. On one day, he described an entire parade as it marched by—with all its floats, cars, and colors. These conversations were the highlight of both their days.

One morning, By-the-door-man woke up and noticed that the room felt different. He looked over toward the window and saw that his friend's bed was empty. When the nurse came into the room he asked what happened to his friend.

"I'm sorry," she said. "He past away very early this morning."

After an appropriate amount of time had past, By-the-door-man requested a bed change. He asked if he could be moved over to the bed by the window, so that he could enjoy the sights his friend had described for him in the prior weeks. Later than same day, his wish was granted, and the beds switched places. "Scoot me as close as you can to the window," he requested with excitement.

As soon as the bed's wheels were locked into place, he used what strength he had to prop himself up on his elbow and peer out the window to the world outside. But to his shock, he could see nothing but a brick wall. He looked from side to side. He wiped his eyes and looked again. Then laid back against his pillow—half disappointed, half amazed.

The next time the nurse came into the room the man asked her to tell him about his friend by the window—the man who had recently died. "Would you believe that guy created a Wonderland for me through this here window. But it turns out, there's nothing there at all."

"Oh," the nurse responded. "That's fascinating. Because your friend by the window was blind."

Your words have the power of life and death. Imagine what is possible if you use your words well.

* * *

I was in a bookstore at an airport not long ago. As I was buying some water at the check-out counter, I overheard a frustrated mother. She grabbed her son and shook his arm until the candy he was clenching fell back into its box.

"Were you going to steal that, boy?"

"No," the boy said in shame.

"I swear, child, you're going to end up in prison someday."

How many troubled young people are simply living up to the words spoken over them by their parents?

Did you know that your words can predict the future?

> *"Tell a man he's brave, and you help him to become so."*
> —Thomas Carlyle

Your words have the power of life and death.

You were created in God's image, and our God speaks things into being.[9] In fact, it is written that it's *God who gives life to the dead and calls into being things that were not.*[10]

How do you speak to yourself?

In the absence of new information, our minds will maintain what's already there. And I know that there's a strong chance that you have words that were spoken to you—or shouted at you—and became imprinted in your mind a long time ago. Words that have shaped how you think about yourself and others. Words that play like tapes, over and over, in your head.

Psychologically, words trigger pictures in the mind, which trigger emotions, which trigger behaviors. You might think you have a behavioral problem, but you might actually have a word problem.

It's time to speak words of life—to yourself.

We hear people say things like, "I'm such an idiot!" or, "I suck!" They think they're being funny or self-deprecating, but they're actually training their expectations. You will behave in the way you believe yourself to be. If you speak negatively of yourself, you'll believe negative things about yourself, and you'll walk those believes into reality. The good news is that the opposite is also true. And while you live in a world that wants to fill your mind with lies to hold you back, the truth is that you're a child of God, created uniquely, for a purpose, and your life matters. In fact, there are all kinds of truths that you should speak to yourself everyday. I've created a short list for you in Appendix 'W'

Give your mind new information. Replace old lies with new truths. Speak yourself into new beliefs and new behaviors.

Your words have the power of life and death.

---

9.   *Genesis 1*

10.   *Romans 4:17 TNIV*

Experiment

....

Question:

What are words that run your mind on a daily basis? What words would help you become the person that you desire to be?

Action:

Choose a few words, quotes, or bible verses and repeat them to yourself all day. Write them in places where you'll see them. Use them to replace old, negative words.

STRONG AND COURAGEOUS

"Courage is the most important of all the virtues, because without courage you can't practice any other virtue consistently. You can practice any virtue erratically, but nothing consistently without courage."
—Maya Angelou

What kind of reminders do you use? Rubber bands on the wrist? Alarms/ alerts in your phone? Sticky notes?

What do you need to be reminded of? Pay the bill…feed the dog…brush your teeth…put on pants…

Sometimes people use notes to remind themselves of things that are true, things they want to believe, words to motivate themselves toward progress and growth.

I went off to college when my younger brother, Josh, was entering his junior year of high school. Josh earned the starting quarterback position his junior year. It was a big deal that Josh was starting as the quarterback, captain, and leader of his team. He took the responsibility seriously and wanted to do his best. Since Josh is a regular human with insecurity and nerves, he found it helpful to call me on Thursday night before the big game on Friday. I was honored to provide what little inspiration I could for my brother from my dorm room an hour away.

The words I used aren't memorable, but I'll tell you what my goal was. I wanted to inspire my brother to be strong and courageous. I wanted him to believe that he belonged there—leading his team, throwing the football. He had prepared, and he had what it took to win. He just needed to keep that truth and belief in his mind.

When we talk about the power of words, we're talking about reminding our-

selves of things that are true. We are easily influenced, prone to doubt and insecurity. We need reminders of who we are and what we believe.

I call it "speaking strength." And I'm going to invite you to speak strength
to yourself. And we're going to start with one small phrase that has empowered
people for thousands of years.

"Be strong and courageous."

* * *

Moses led the Israelites out of slavery in Egypt, through the Red Sea, and
into the desert on their way to the Promised Land. But as close to God as Moses
had been, God chose Joshua (a name sharing the same root and pointing to the
eventual Savior, "Jesus") to lead the people into the Promised Land. Let's stop
here and consider this cosmic shift in leadership.

> *And Moses the servant of the LORD died there in Moab,
> as the LORD had said...8 The Israelites grieved for Moses
> in the plains of Moab thirty days, until the time of weeping
> and mourning was over.*
>
> *⁹ Now Joshua son of Nun was filled with the spirit of
> wisdom because Moses had laid his hands on him. So
> the Israelites listened to him and did what the LORD had
> commanded Moses.*
>
> *¹⁰ Since then, no prophet has risen in Israel like Moses,
> whom the LORD knew face to face, ¹¹ who did all those
> signs and wonders the LORD sent him to do in Egypt—to
> Pharaoh and to all his officials and to his whole land. ¹² For
> no one has ever shown the mighty power or performed
> the awesome deeds that Moses did in the sight of all
> Israel. —Deuteronomy 34*

That's how Deuteronomy closes. That's who Joshua has to follow. No one
was greater. No one has been greater since. And yet here is Joshua, tasked with
the responsibility to be impossibly great and do what Moses was not able to do.

How would you respond if God asked you to replace Moses as the leader? I
suggest that you would respond in one of a few ways:

- You've got the wrong person
- You've got the wrong assignment, or
- It's about time you noticed!

In our "everybody gets a trophy" generation, it's not absurd to believe that there might be some level of "it's about time you noticed" entitlement. Perhaps you're waiting for a promotion. Maybe you've been overlooked in the past. Maybe others are receiving opportunities that you're not. Maybe you're just young and think you're more ready than you are.

Hear this now: Entitlement will ruin your life. If you want to reach the places you envision for yourself, you need to let go of the entitlement of knowing how you'll get there. If you want to lead a team, an organization, or a community, you need to make sure you're about the people and not about your position. You'll ruin your life striving for a role, and if you got it, you'd ruin the lives of others with your self-centeredness.

Fortunately for the Israelites, Joshua didn't have an attitude of entitlement.

He was, however, afraid. Here are fears he likely experienced. Pause and ask yourself in what ways you can relate.

- **Fear of failure** – There will be real battles, real tests, real pain. Everyone will look to me. I've never done this before. The stakes are high.
- **Fear of future** – Will God keep coming through—for me? He came through in the past, but the past is the past. What if I screw something up and the future isn't like the past? What if the future is a disappointment?
- **Fear of following (Moses)** – I'm not like him. He had different gifts that me. He was stronger in areas that seem important. He was a living legend. I'm just a guy.
- **Fear of not being followed** – I don't want to look stupid. I don't want to feel alone. I don't want to look back and realize that no one's coming with me.

These kinds of fears can paralyze us and make us quit before we even begin. And if we quit, we'll likely try and talk ourselves out of the opportunity with things that don't sound like fear. We might become critical of other people and make it about them. "The people are whiners. They barely followed Moses. This is a disaster in the making." We'll compare ourselves to others and look for easy out "Moses: I'm not like him." Or we get caught up in the past and take our eyes off the new thing that God is doing in the present.

It's normal. But it's not okay. This is what God said to Joshua:

Have I not commanded you? Be strong and courageous.
Do not be afraid; do not be discouraged, for the LORD your
God will be with you wherever you go.
—Joshua 1:9

Be strong and courageous! The Lord is leading. The God of the Universe will be with you. Don't be afraid.

Fear is a natural part of life, but you serve a supernatural God. It's time to remind yourself of things that are true. Things that are in front of you.

You need to continue *speaking strength* to yourself.

Experiment

Question:

Where in your life is God inviting you into a future that requires courage?

Action:

Make a declaration. When I took over the church I lead in Huntington Beach, it was not in great shape. There was a clear risk of failure. But, unlike other times in my life, I decided to commit fully. I would give it everything I had. If it failed, it would fail with my best efforts.

The decision was made, but it wasn't enough for only me to believe. I needed others to understand my level of commitment, because I needed others onboard. I talked about my commitment often and in different ways. I cast vision of the desired future, and I showed people that I believed it by moving my family into the community. "We're here. This is going to work. Believe it. And join us."

Make the declaration. Rally the troops.

And tell yourself over and over, "Be strong and courageous!"

For additional Tips on Speaking Strength, see Appendix S

TEACHABLE

The wise realize that they can learn something from anyone.

I recently attended a leadership seminar where a former president was interviewed. Because of this president's track record and political positions, there were more than a few people in the room who were grossly turned off by the thought of learning from him. A number of people protested the session and stood outside, in essence saying, "We are disappointed that this man was included in the leadership event."

What the protesters were really saying was, "We are too prejudiced, proud, and self-righteous to learn anything from this speaker." The protesters who didn't attend the event missed out on a very humble and insightful interview with a man who has much to offer in the ways of leading people.

I regret my days in school when I sat bored and inattentive in numerous classrooms. Looking back, I'm sure there was so much more I could've learned had I tried. I'm sure each teacher was a wealth of information in some way, on some subject—had I cared enough to discover the value of his or her experience.

Besides the value of being a lifelong learner, there is also value in considering oneself a "teacher." You, too, have valuable experiences. No one has lived the life you have lived. That makes you more of an expert on your experiences and insights than anyone else. You understand things that I don't. I understand things that you don't. Even someone with no education living in a grass hut on the opposite side of the world could teach us immensely about some aspect of life—if we cared enough to listen, and to learn.

Here are just a few simple things that help ongoing learners:

1.   Ask a lot of questions
2.   Consider each person's uniqueness
3.   Determine what subjects bring the person to life
4.   Seek to learn something every day
5.   Ask God for more wisdom

> *If any of you lacks wisdom, you should ask God,*
> *who gives generously to all without finding fault,*
> *and it will be given to you. —James 1:5*

God wants to give you wisdom. The rub is that you need to be willing to receive it, even if the wisdom—truth—is inconvenient.

Often, wisdom is less about new information and more about *reframing* old ideas. We talked about "attitude" and "outlook" in previous chapters, but "reframing" is a similar tool that could dramatically change your life.

My father-in-law and brother-in-law are in construction. They are good at what they do. My father-in-law built his own house from the ground up, which stands in stark contrast to my inability to put together Ikea furniture.

I saw one of their projects—before and after. It started as a small and unimpressive house. The main floor was broken up by walls that made the living room feel small and the kitchen feel separate and enclosed. But when they were done, it was a completely different house. I felt like I was walking into an HGTV episode, complete with "oos" and "awes". It's amazing what you can do when you know how to reframe a home.

It's amazing what you can do in your life if you learn to reframe your beliefs and experiences.

Before I went through a divorce, I judged divorced people. How could they let that happen? They couldn't even keep their most important relationship together? How could they lead others?

Oh, wait…now that's me. Perhaps I need to reframe my beliefs and snap judgments.

I don't like cats. I grew up allergic. Whether that was a physical reality or an emotional conviction, I was allergic to four-legged, marble-eyed spawn of the devil. That is, until my wife lost her mom to cancer, leaving the family reeling and my wife despondent. My mother-in-law had a cat. It was Hilary's when she was younger. So, now the cat was ours. And I've done my best.

Some issues become more clear in a different light. Convictions we once held are loosened. Biases and prejudices are a put aside when new realities are realized.

Here's a hunch: You have some beliefs, biases, preferences, and points of view that you have held onto for dear life, but in light of life and death…they're silly. You may have lost friends over your desire to be right. You may have ostracized others over convictions that are not the "main things."

Jesus was constantly challenging the convictions of religious people who were convinced that they were right. His message was of love, not being right or better.[11] Time and time again He reframed their self-righteous beliefs and self-serving perspectives. *"You have heard that it was said, 'You shall not commit adultery.' But I tell you that anyone who looks at a woman lustfully has already committed adultery with her in his heart.*[12] There were many in that day and in our day who judge the obvious "sinners" while possessing the same lust, deceit, and ugliness in their own hearts and heads. Jesus seems to say, reframe your belief system—and change your heart.

If you become handicapped, you look at handicapped people differently. If you go through a divorce, you change your judgmental attitude toward divorced people. When you get laid off, you have new empathy for those temporarily out of the workforce. Difficult circumstances and events have a way of reframing and refocusing your outlook on life.

But what if it didn't take pain? What if you could learn from a Significant Learning Moment instead of a Significant Life Event? What if you could reframe your perspective and add a little love to your life without the rude awakening?

Stay humble. Stay teachable.

Humility = Teachability

---

11.   *Matt 22*

12.   *Matt 5:27-28*

Experiment

Question:
Who in your life right now could teach you more than you are allowing him or her to teach you? What negative or judgmental attitudes, beliefs, or perspectives need reframing?

Action:
Think of someone whom you see regularly, but rarely take the time to engage on a meaningful level. Seek them out and ask them questions. Listen to understand. Drive the conversation toward finding something that is significant to that person. Discover what makes them tick and why they are who they are. Learn from them.

ADD VALUE

*"Try not to become a person of success,
but a person of value."*
—Albert Einstein

I was listening to the radio this week and heard about a young man named Robert. Robert has a mysterious sickness that has taken over his body to the extent that he's lost control of his faculties. His situation has deteriorated mysteriously and quickly. Short of divine intervention, Robert will not get healthy. The doctors are certain that Robert's body is shutting down and that he will die. The doctors thought that he'd have given in by now, but he continues to fight.

"I could just roll over and die," Robert said, "but I need to keep on."

Robert also said that he expects to live several more months and that several months from now he'll be further along and will have contributed more to the world than if he simply gave up today.

Robert is adding value to the world around him. Even though he's on the verge of death without most bodily functions, he's still making the world a better place.

Robert can relate to the Apostle Paul who I paraphrase, "I'm on the verge of death, and I'd rather die, because the next life will be better by far, yet there is more for me to contribute in this life. By fighting to stay alive, I can encourage many others. That, then, is what I will do."[13]

* * *

13. *Philippians 1*

In theory, I encourage people for a living. I help people think about their lives and consider their Creator and what He would say about their lives. But this wasn't my first job.

My first job was selling Cutco knives one summer as a teenager. That gig, like many, was both brilliant and brutal. Brutal because I cold-called people and went to their home to sell them knives. But it was brilliant because the knives are fantastic (I still have and use my starter set), and because I got to sit in people's homes. Even though I was a teenager, I was amazed at how people would open up and talk about their lives. I didn't only sell knives. I listened to people, and I encouraged people.

Being a knives salesman might seem like a lame job, but only if you're just a knife salesman. I was a need-meeter. People had an immediate need—food needs cutting. They also had unspoken needs—desire for connection, to be heard, to feel like they were helping a young man in his first job. I wasn't a knife salesman. I was a problem-solver that genuinely cared about the person.

Similarly, my friend Ryan doesn't view himself as an insurances salesman. He brings security and confidence to people's lives around the areas that are the most sensitive.

Cecilia isn't just a hairstylist. She elevates not only her customer's look, but their esteem every time they sit in her chair.

Randy is not just an e-commerce entrepreneur. He prides himself in creating pathways and connections for new relationships and opportunities.

What about you? What do you do? Or, a better question, how do you leverage your work to add value to the lives of people?

* * *

"The way out is through."
—Robert Frost

Maybe you're still discouraged and feeling stuck, vocationally. A lot of people get stuck in life because they are looking for a way out—something else, something other, to alleviate their pain, dissatisfaction, or boredom. They assume that different circumstances would fix their vocational issues. And they might be right. But most people make a terrible mistake: They look for shortcuts and escape hatches instead of doing excellent work where they are.

People who do their jobs with passion, energy, and creativity quickly find themselves in higher and higher demand—being promoted and offered "better" jobs. The best way out is through.

People who complain or quit become less attractive to a world looking for value-adders.

When I began to be asked to play a "consultant" role for a couple different organizations, I asked an excellent consultant to mentor me in the most important elements of his work.

"Add value," he said. "Figure out what makes you unique, what you do best, and how what you do can best serve this organization…and do that with excellence."

You can follow this logic to earnings. Most people are looking for an hourly or monthly wage. Instead, people who begin to understand the unique value that they bring begin to look at the benefit they offer to a person or organization they are serving. They don't set a rate or charge based upon time spent, but value contributed. If the customer is deriving great value, they should pay the consultant well for the benefits they are deriving. If the consultant doesn't deliver value, the customer shouldn't have to pay.

A professional golfer was struggling with his golf swing. He went from consistently finishing in the top 10 and winning tournaments to failing to make the cut—not even getting into tournaments. His earnings were falling, his caddy was leaving, and the golfer was desperate. So he hired a golf coach known for refining the swings of great players. The coach worked with the golfer everyday for a month leading up to the one of the biggest tournaments of the year. The golf swing came back, and better than ever. The golfer won the tournament, earning him over one million dollars.

Two weeks later, the golfer got the bill from the coaching. The bill was for $100,000 plus expenses. The golfer called the coach and left a message that went something like this:

"Hey coach… I don't want to sound ungrateful, because you obviously helped me a ton, but $100,000 seems like a lot for four weeks of coaching. My manager and accountant are going to want a little explanation for the charge. Thanks."

Another week passed and the golfer received a revised bill from the coach. It read:

Four weeks of coaching	*$20,000*
Knowing how to coach a champion	*$80,000*
Total	*$100,000*

When you get results, you get paid.

For many in our everyone-gets-a-trophy culture, this results-oriented reality is a rude awakening. But it doesn't have to be. You have something to contribute to this world. It might not be golf-coaching, but it is something. Find your unique contribution and make it great. Even if your job doesn't seem great, be great in your job. When you add value, you *feel* valuable.

And when you hit a rough patch, don't quit and don't complain. Power through it. Do your very best, even if you think no one's watching. Someone's always watching.

> *Whatever you do, work at it with all your heart,*
> *as working for the Lord...*
> —Colossians 3:23

One of the greatest things you can do with your life is to contribute to the lives of others. You don't have to be famous or fancy. You don't have to be rich or in charge. Wherever you find yourself, add value. Start now. Do your best, and good things will happen.

And remember the words of Maya Angelou:

> *"I have learned that people will forget what you said, people will forget what you did, but people will never forget how you made them feel."*

Experiment

Question:
How could you redefine your job—at least in your own mind—and turn your efforts into more passion and meaning?

Action:
Regardless of your role or title, write down your own job description. Decide who you want to be and what you want to contribute. Now begin to approach each day with that mindset.

Opportunity comes to those who make the most of the opportunities they already have.

WINNING

> *"As you walk down the fairway of life you must smell the roses,*
> *for you only get to play one round."*
> —Ben Hogan

My friend Cliff is a legendary volleyball personality in the greater Seattle area. He is 55 years old and still the ringleader of the small sub-culture of men's beach volleyball players in the area. Twenty years ago, he was one of the best players, winning most of the tournaments he entered. At 55, he's still tough to beat.

There are a couple of secrets to Cliff's lasting success in the Northwest beach volleyball scene.

1. Don't stop playing. Cliff has never taken more than a month off at a time. And he plays three or four days a week. He went so far as to build a state-of-the-art sand court in his front yard. I was willing to drive an hour both ways just to play at Cliff's.

There's a lot to be said for simply being consistent. Even if you don't have the natural physical abilities of others, if you refuse to give up, you'll eventually achieve a high level.

2. Treat sport as play. Volleyball is still a childlike passion for Cliff. Even though he is a great player, and has had tremendous success, it's still just a game. He doesn't take himself or the sport too seriously. Now don't get me wrong. Every single game Cliff plays—even at 55 years old—he tries to win. But win or lose, he plays because he enjoys it.

Many parents and coaches have taken the fun out of sports for too many kids. Without realizing it, they are shaping kids' futures—not only in sports, but in many aspects of competitive life.

Volleyball was almost ruined for me in college. I didn't play the sport for two years after finishing with the team. Why? It wasn't fun anymore. I was playing at the Division One level, but I wasn't satisfied because I wasn't enjoying it. I took the game too seriously.

Not long ago, I was at Cliff's house playing beach volleyball. Cliff asked me if I'd be playing in the upcoming tournament. I told him I didn't think I wanted to travel and make the effort because I hadn't won any tournaments this summer thus far. Without a quality partner, I had no chance of winning this one.

"You know," Cliff responded, "if there was a switch, like a light switch, and I could flick it one way and win every single tournament, never losing…or, I could flick it the other way, never win a tournament, but always have fun playing volleyball, I'd take having fun, no question. It's not worth winning if you're wound so tight you can't enjoy it. I try to just live in the moment." And here's the ironic thing: Cliff wins… a lot. There's something about playing loose and free that produces good results.

I need regular reminders that life is short. Live. Play. Enjoy.

"The true object of all human life is play.
Earth is a task garden; heaven is a playground."
—GK Chesterton

Experiment

....

Question:

In what ways are you too worried about outcomes and not enjoying the journey?

Action:

Play today. And play for fun. Let winning be a bonus.

CHRISTMAS EVERYDAY

"The gift is to the giver, and comes back to him..."
—Walt Whitman

I'm a crier. Yes, television, movies...good news articles...Here's one I just read and had to wipe my cheeks through.

The young father stood in line at the Kmart layaway counter, wearing dirty clothes and worn-out boots. With him were three small children.

He asked to pay something on his bill because he knew he wouldn't be able to afford it all before Christmas. Then a mysterious woman stepped up to the counter.

"She told him, 'No, I'm paying for it,'" recalled Edna Deppe, assistant manager at the store in Indianapolis. "He just stood there and looked at her and then looked at me and asked if it was a joke. I told him it wasn't, and that she was going to pay for him. And he just busted out in tears."

At Kmart stores across the country, Santa seems to be getting some help: Anonymous donors are paying off strangers' layaway accounts, buying the Christmas gifts other families couldn't afford, especially toys and children's clothes set aside by impoverished parents.

Before she left the store Tuesday evening, the Indianapolis woman in her mid-40s had paid the layaway orders for as many as 50 people. On the way out, she handed out $50 bills and paid for two carts of toys for a woman in line at the cash register.

"She was doing it in the memory of her husband who had just died, and she said she wasn't going to be able to spend it and wanted to make people happy with it," Deppe said. The woman did not identify herself and only asked people to "remember Ben," an apparent reference to her husband.

Deppe, who said she's worked in retail for 40 years, had never seen anything like it.

"It was like an angel fell out of the sky and appeared in our store," she said.[14]

The Kmart employee called the generous woman an angel. She wasn't an angel. She was someone who *gets it*. Someone like you.

This woman doesn't know it, but she inspired me. Now she's inspiring you. Obviously, she enhanced Christmas for 50+ people and their families, but her act of generosity has reached much further than Indianapolis. This story has traveled the globe. And I found it worth telling again here.

The generous woman didn't know about *My Near Death Experiment* when she went to Kmart that day, yet she embodied it. After losing her husband—one of the most painful experiences one can have in life—she shifted the focus off herself, off her grief, and off her lack and she went into action. She turned her tragedy into a blessing for many. And many others—including my wife and I—have acted along with this woman for the sake of others who have less.

And now it's your turn…

It may or may not be the Christmas season when you're reading this. It doesn't matter. You can embody the generous spirit of Christmas any day, and everyday.

Why do we store up acts of kindness for the holidays? People are hurting year-round. There are stories around you right now. A family in need that you're not even aware of. People in your neighborhood, in your apartment complex, in your workplace…People living a nightmare. They just got bad news. They just lost a loved one. Their health is failing again. They might not need toys, but they could use something. And that something is going to come through you.

True generosity is uncommon. The normal, expected thing is to look out for yourself. But it's shocking, compelling, and life-giving when you put someone else ahead of yourself.[15]

* * *

One of the first words you learned as a child was "mine!" And you should spend the rest of your life breaking your grip.

There are two primary things that prevent us from living generous lives: entitlement and distraction.

---

14.   http://finance.yahoo.com/news/anonymous-donors-pay-off-kmart-222535611.html;

       By Margery a. Beck, Associated Press | AP

15.   Luke 14:14

Distraction because we're so preoccupied with our own lives and our own needs that we miss the needs around us.

Entitlement because we somehow believe that we deserve what we have—actually, that we deserve more. This mentality is a scarcity paradigm—that there is not enough to go around and I've got to get mine. The scarcity paradigm promotes selfishness. But a paradigm of abundance believes that God has all the resources and there's enough to go around.

Why is it that a bird sings? It doesn't know where its next meal will come from. But a worm-shortage isn't on its mind. A bird doesn't care that we're in a bad economy. The bird knows that its Creator has always made sure it's fed, and it doesn't question whether or not that will be true tomorrow.

Look at the birds of the air; they do not sow or reap or store away in barns, and yet your heavenly Father feeds them. Are you not much more valuable than they? —Matthew 6:6

Don't worry whether you have enough. Don't concern yourself if someone else has more.

Jealousy is counting the blessings of others instead of your own.

Be thankful. Be generous. Enjoy the fact that you're provided for, and provide for someone else.

Experiment

Question:

What prevents you from being generous?

Action:

Do an act of generosity today or tomorrow. Here are a few ideas:

- Hand out flowers to complete strangers.
- Buy the dinner of the people next to you.
- Distribute a bouquet of $20 bills.
- Fill up someone else's gas tank.
- Sponsor a child in another country.
- Call your city officials. (It's easy. Do an internet search for the "city of...." Call the number during office hours—preferably in the morning.) Ask what the biggest needs in the city are. Do something about one.

FORGIVENESS

The Rejection Rule: *You will be rejected. Guaranteed.*

Sorry if that's a rude awakening for you. But it's true. You can't live long in this life without experiencing rejection, hurt, and pain. The old adage is true: hurt people hurt people. And you will inevitably fall on both sides of that equation.

I remember being on the blacktop of Condit Elementary School at lunch time. I was playing basketball, and I was playing well—one of the better 5th grade basketball prospects, if I do so say. You could recognize me for my long legs and my long hair. The hair was my own in interpretation of Zach Morris from Saved by the Bell. And it was popular. My mom even had other soccer moms approach her during games asking about my trend-setting hair. "When do you think Caleb will cut his hair," one mom asked. "I'm ready for Steve to cut his."

But that day, on the blacktop, things changed for me. What had been the popular, trend-setting style, was in question. Not to my face, mind you, but while I ran up the court I could hear one of my friends say to another kid, "How long is Caleb going to let his hair get? He's starting to look like a girl."

I was devastated. I went home and asked my mom to make a haircut appointment that same day.

In the years since, the pain I've experienced has increased in intensity—from negative coaches, to jealous friends, to judgmental Christians. Even our parents—as much as they want to protect us from pain, they are often the cause of it.

One of the famously shocking statements of Jesus was this one: *Then Peter came to him and asked, "Lord, how often should I forgive someone who sins against me? Seven times?" "No, not seven times," Jesus replied, "but seventy times seven!*[16]

In other words, be willing to forgive to a ridiculous extent. That doesn't mean we don't create boundaries. You don't have trust or hang out with people who hurt you. But you must forgive them.

The scriptures teach that if you don't extend grace, a bitter root will grow with you.[17] A bitter root has a way of twisting itself around your heart and soul, suffocating your joy, your fun, your life. You see, many people choose not to forgive, and hold offenses against the offender. But what they seldom realize is that they are, in effect, holding *themselves* imprisoned to their own bitterness.

Consider these Forgiveness Myths:

1. If I forgive I'm not being honest or true to myself.

2. If I forgive I'll be letting the offender "off the hook."

---

16. *Matthew 18:21-22*

17. *Hebrew 12:14-15*

3. If I forgive I'm inviting the person to hurt me again.

4. By not forgiving I can stay in control—in the position of power.

These concerns are simply untrue. The truth is that unforgiveness is hurting *you* more than anyone else.

* * *

In Matthew 18, Jesus tells the story of king who wanted to settle accounts. There was a businessman who owed the king millions of dollars. Given the state of the economy, the king was calling the loan and asked the businessman to pay the debt off. The man couldn't, and protocol was to have the man thrown into prison until his family and business associates could come up with the millions owed. But the man begged and pleaded with king, "Have mercy! I'm good for it. It's just a bad economy."

So the king did have mercy. Radical mercy, in fact. He forgave the debt entirely—wiping it clean.

The same businessman who had been shown unprecedented mercy was walking the marketplace soon after. He came across anther man who owed him a few hundred dollars. The recently pardoned businessman made a direct path for the other owing him a minor debt. And when he confronted him, he grabbed the man by the throat, shook him, and demanded his money. The man owing the small debt begged the businessman. "Please, have mercy. I have a wife and kids. I'll get you the money soon. It's a bad economy." But the businessman showed the debtor no mercy. Instead, he had the man thrown into prison until he could pay every cent.

The king had people on the street, and they saw what the businessman had done. Just after being forgiven a debt of millions of dollars, the man had the nerve to choke another guy out for a few hundred. The king was outraged. He had the businessman brought back into his presence and he let him have it.

"I forgive you for this massive debt. And you couldn't forgive your friend for a small debt? You're wicked and corrupt. And you'll spend the rest of your life in prison until you can back every penny that you owe me."

When Jesus told parables they always had a deeper meaning than what was obvious on the surface. This parable is a parable about money. And this parable is NOT a parable about money.

Jesus was describing the generous forgiveness of God. His point is clear: God has forgiven you and me an unthinkable debt. We're the million-dollar debtor. It's you. And it's me. We owe Him more than we could ever repay, and He cleaned our slate.

God is a God of generosity. His radical forgiveness is an extension of his generosity toward us.

How, then, could we justify holding anything against another person?

You must make allowance for each other's faults and forgive the person who offends you. Remember, the Lord forgave you, so you must forgive others. —Colossians 3:13 (NLT)

Here are a few things that will help you come to grips with forgiveness:

1. **Identify with the offender.**

   Our tendency is to say, "I'm not like that person. He's a cheater. I just fudge my taxes because the government is corrupt. She's a gossip. I just talk about her because people need to understand that she's poisonous."

   The Apostle Paul said, "I am the worst of sinners."[18] I've come to a similar conclusion. I figure that I'm capable of anything. Under the right circumstances, I doubt there's a sin I wouldn't commit. If I'd grown up that way, I'd have probably made even worse decisions. If I was abused like that, I'd likely be even more messed up. You get it.

2. **Surrender the right to repayment.**

   You can't afford to get even. It's too costly to your soul. The longer you carry the burden, the darker your heart will become. The more you lust for revenge and retribution, the more you miss out on the best of life in the present. *May the Lord judge between you and me. And may the Lord avenge the wrongs you have done to me, but my hand will not touch you.*[19]

   The guy who clings to his bitterness or holds onto resentment like a badge of honor is only making matters worse. His life is like Groundhog's day, repeating the same emotional burdens day after day; rehashing the incident; playing it over in his mind; rehearsing his "f-you" speech. He's stuck. And though he's in denial, he's miserable.

   Remember, the King owns it all. So release your sense of entitlement. Let it go. And go forward.

3. **Pray for the offender to be blessed.**

   This is the final forgiveness test. If you can genuinely pray for God to bless the person who hurt you, you have released the offense—you have fully forgiven.

---

18.   *1 Timothy 1:16*

19.   *1 Samuel 24:12*

Believe me, I understand that your pain is real and probably severe. But no matter what the offense, you're only torturing yourself if you don't forgive. Forgiveness unlocks your healing.

Experiment

Questions:
Who have you been unable to pray for God to bless?

Action:
Walk yourself through the three steps above. Pray that God would allow you to experience His grace…and then offer than same grace to others who hurt you.

Be kind and compassionate to one another,
forgiving each other, just as in Christ God forgave you.
—Ephesians 4:32

LEAN INTO THE KNIFE

Many are the plans in a person's heart,
but it is the Lord's purpose that prevails.
—Proverbs: 19-21

During my period of quarter-life crisis I received some advice from a friend that I'll never forget. He told me to *lean into the knife.*

This friend knew my desire to move quickly past the embarrassment of my circumstances, and move back to full-throttle, fast-pace, and maximum impact. He understood the human nature that wants to put pain and humiliation behind us quickly and move to better feelings and a sense of progress. But the lessons I was learning are lessons best learned once. I don't want to have to repeat that life course. So, in light of making the most of my pain, I attempted to lean into the knife.

I didn't ignore my problems or lie about the deeper issues. I allowed others to help me identify "blind spots" in my character and worldview, that are much easier to ignore. I worked a humble job, and lived in a modest way. Looking back, it might have been the most valuable season of my life. But when I was in it I didn't like it.

Be in the season you're in. If you're in a hurry to move on to the next season of life, you'll miss the lessons you need to learn in this season. Not only will you miss the learnings, you'll miss the joys, the laughs, the divine moments, and the key relationships. Be here, now.

When you lean into the knife you accept pain. You refuse to numb, and choose not to run. Instead, you let the Master Physician take the scalpel to the areas of your life that are dead and in decay—the parts of you that are hurting the rest of you.

But sharp pain today saves you from worse pain in the future. When you allow the Spiritual Surgeon to have His way, you're actually choosing a life of health instead of creeping disease. A life of honesty instead self-deception. A life of feeling instead of shallow numbness.

Lean into the knife.

Learn all the lessons you can learn from your present circumstances. Don't avoid or deny current realities. They will come back to haunt you later.

Be in the season you're in. Don't race on to the next chapter. Don't jump into the next relationship. Learn whatever you can learn right now. Don't repeat destructive patterns. Choose the honest present.

Experiment

Questions:
What circumstance or season have you tried to avoid or race through?

Action:
Stop distracting yourself. Stop avoiding the reality. Decide right now that you will not miss the lessons of this season of life because you are in such a hurry to get to the next season. Consider going to a counselor to see what they draw out of you.

NEGU

"Perseverance is not a long race;
it is many short races one after the other."
—Walter Elliot

My first job out of college was across the street from LA Fitness. I walked (well, sadly, I mostly drove—American) across the street and played basketball at lunch two days a week. Me and nine other midday glory seekers would battle it out on the hardwood floors of that LA Fitness, reliving some childhood fantasy of elite athleticism. It wasn't pretty. One guy always wore goggles. Another was famous for his long socks and headband. There was the compulsive cusser, the defensive enforcer who needed to lighten up, the insecure guy who always tried to pick the teams so he wasn't selected last, the young quick kid who always seemed to outrun his skill level, and the occasional girl who loved that she could hold her own with the guys. And then there was Erik.

Erik was in his mid-thirties during this era of "sandlot" basketball. Erik is just under six feet and, though you'd never guess it, he struggled with his weight as a younger man. Not any more. The guy is a machine. I remember in those days that he arrived at work at the same early hour everyday. He played basketball across the street four days a week, lifted weights right before playing, and ate healthy foods. His fitness and health regimen inspired me. His basketball game, however, was the most impressive.

Erik ran circles around the other sweaty, panting, wanna-be athletes on the court. He never stopped moving. Active hands on defense, sprinting down the court, running off ignorant screens…even diving on the floor for loose balls…at LA Fitness! But the attribute he's most famous for is his ability to make shots from literally anywhere inside of half court. I would think I was guarding him well, up-close, moving my feet, fighting off screens…but he always managed to get a shot off—and it usually went in. If Erik caught fire, he'd hit four consecutive deep shots, worth double points, and you'd find yourself down 8 - 0. It was frustrating to play against him, but impressive to watch.

Erik earned the nickname, "Energizer Bunny," because he just kept going. He never stopped. He never seemed to get tired. And he never quit. I remember one game where he missed his first six or seven shots in a row. His team was losing. Teammates were getting frustrated. But Erik just worked even harder. More intensity on defense, more activity on offense…and eventually he started making shots. After missing his first six or seven shots, he made the next seven in a row, and his team won by one point. I knew he had to be excited about the comeback, but you couldn't tell by his face. It was just business as usual.

I told you everything above to tell you this…

My friend Erik—as great as he is—is not the most impressive person in his family. Erik's 12-year-old daughter, Jessica Joy Rees, has inspired literally hundreds of thousands of people. Let her inspire you…

As I write this chapter, it's the week following the celebration of the life of Jessica (Jessie) Joy Rees. You've heard these events generally referred to as funerals, but Jessie's was a celebration. Jessie died a week before her party, at 12-years-old, after a year-long fight with cancer. The week following her transition to heaven, her family hosted a celebration of Jessie's life at their home church: Saddleback

Church in Lake Forrest, CA. Over 3,400 people turned out for the event, and hundreds more watched live online from all over the country and around the world. I've never witnessed anything like it. It was an incredible tragedy—a precious 12-year-old girl being snatched from her family just as her life story was beginning to unfold. And while there was definite sadness, there was parallel joy, inspiration, and optimism. There was an energy that suggested we were all going to live better lives because of Jessie's example.

In the last ten months of Jessie's life, she devoted her time—when she wasn't dealing with her countless treatments and procedures—to encouraging other children with cancer. In spite of an aggressive brain cancer that would claim vision, hearing, and motor functions, Jessie kept the faith, and kept her focus on others. With the help of her parents, she founded an organization called NEGU: *Never Ever Give Up*.

You can go the website to learn more (NEGU.org), but one of Jessie's goals was to see the number of "Likes" on her Facebook page reach the 50,000 mark. In just a few short months the number went from 0 to 56,000 before she died. Today, just weeks later, it's 150,000. Go to Facebook and find Jessie Rees Foundation and see what's happened since.

Jessie leveraged the exponential popularity of her Facebook fan page to talk about other kids with cancer. She asked her fans to pray for every sick child she learned of from the Children's Hospital, and any kid with cancer that messaged her for support.

Jessie had an idea she called "Joy Jars," filled with small things that kids would like when they are stuck in hospital beds. She assembled the jars herself until she ran out of energy. Thousands of Joy Jars have been distributed. UPS agreed to support the delivery effort. And the momentum is just getting started. Jessie has sparked a flame that will continue to burn. In just 12 short years, she lived in such a way that her legacy will endure for years to come. Jessie took tragedy and leveraged it for good…for others.

At the celebration of Jessie's life, her best friend Sophia wrote, "We had hoped for a miracle. When she left us, we realized that she was the miracle."

Jessie never gave up despite months of miserable pain on the sobering road to the great unknown…and yet she still died. Why? Why do bad things happen to good people? Why do good things happen to bad people? As confusing, devastating, and heart-wrenching as loss is, there is a larger story at play.

NEGU—never ever give up—extends beyond this frail life into the eternal. Lives well-lived echo throughout history and help point us toward better living.

Jessie's battle cry was "NEGU." Yet Jessie's battle is over. Her pain is gone. Her body is restored. And her spirit soars.

The question is, what will be *your* battle cry?

Experiment

Question:

Where do you need to persevere and not give up?

Action:

Write down the words "Never Ever Give Up" somewhere you need to see them. Now, continue to persevere, and leave a legacy of your own.

ENDING AND BEGINNING

"As you grow older, you'll find that many things you regret are the things you didn't do."
—Zachary Scott

You know how they say that we remember or retain less than 10% of what we hear in lectures? Kind of depressing when I think about how much time I spent in plastic chairs listening to teachers and professors pour out their life's knowledge. But some of the things I've learned from teachers or speakers still ring in my ears.

"Ask not what your country can do for you, ask what you can do for your country." —FDR

"Be the change you want to see in the world."—Ghandi

"I have a dream…" –Martin Luther King Jr.

But there's one more in particular that I want to talk about here: "Begin with the end in mind."—Doug Fields at a high school graduation, quoting Stephen Covey.

At a high school graduation it's difficult to pay attention. My buddy next to me is naked under his robe. My family in the stadium seating are sweating and trying to decide what restaurant we can all get into for dinner. And most the people who get on stage have a love-hate relationship with the student-body.

But more than 15 years later, I still remember one sentence from that short message about preparing for the rest of our lives. It was, "Begin with the end in mind."

We will all die. That day is coming. You don't know the day or the hour. But the mortality rate for humans is 100%.

Consider our journey for a moment. In light of our core commitments, values, health, connectedness, gratitude, and our understanding of God and His plan, we re-orient ourselves each day, each hour, each moment to live with attention to what makes us most alive, and what adds the most value to others and to the world around us. And in doing so, we begin to enjoy life…life to the full.

Experiment

Question:

In what situation right now do you need this longer-term perspective?

When it comes to your life going forward, how could you benefit from continuing to live in light of Your Near Death Experiment?

Action:

Begin with the end in mind, and make the next right decision.

DEATH CONTRACT

Knowledge is not power. But when knowledge is applied and shared it becomes powerful.

Death, I'm not afraid of you. I know you're coming for me, but you have no power. You have lost your sting.[20]

In fact, I'm using you. I'm using your haunting reality to make the most of today, and tomorrow. I'm using you to remember the things that matter most. I'm using you to embrace a life of meaning and purpose, because I refuse to go through the motions and waste my time.

Time is precious. Time is a gift. So is my life.

Death, you have been dealt with. I believe in a God of life. Not only is this God the Giver of life, He is the Sustainer of life, and He is the One who has overcome *you*. What, then, is there left to fear?[21]

So I'm on a mission. A mission to maximize the life I've been given. A mission to honor the God who is the Giver of life. A mission to love and serve people and leave a lasting imprint for the good of others.

To fulfill that mission, I'm leveraging death. I'm doing that by remembering and acting upon the convictions I've uncovered through this journey—*My Near Death Experiment.*

Here are my commitments:

20.   *1 Corinthians 15:55*

21.   *Psalm 27:1*

These are the things that matter most to me—my highest priorities around which I organize my life:

This is the authentic manner in which I want to live:

These are some values that will help me stay focused:

This is what *health* looks like for my life:

This is what I want for my outlook and attitude:

This how I'm going to prioritize my relationships:

These are the ways I stay grounded in the *present*—appreciating today—while still creating a better a future:

Let it be so.

_____

(sign)

FINAL THOUGHTS

In the end, you can only enjoy your life if you enjoy yourself. Not your future self that accomplishes great things. Your self right now. You're the only you that will ever be. And you were created, on purpose, by a God who loves you. And the only way to live a life full of purpose and meaning is to receive that love and then pass it on…

Life is simple. Not easy, but simple. May God bless yours.

APPENDIX

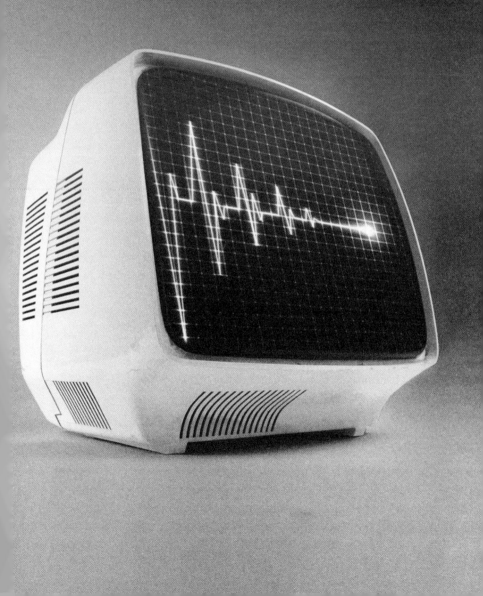

APPENDIX S

Tips for Speaking Strength

1. **Personal:** Write personally (include the world "I")
2. **Positive:** Envision what you want to see happen (state it positively and confidently)
3. **Present:** Write in the present tense ("I am")
4. **Powerful:** Use words that trigger positive emotions
5. **Particular:** Use words that suggest consistency and regularity ("I always…")
6. **Precise:** State specific desires and convictions

APPENDIX W

God's life-giving words

-   God is please with how He made me (Gen 1:31)
-   I am God's masterpiece (Eph 2:10)
-   I am a child of God (John 1:12)
-   I have been adapted as God's child (Eph 1:7)
-   The spirit of God is in me (I Cor 3:16)
-   Jesus calls me friend (John 15:15)
-   I am a member of the body of Christ (1 Cor 12:27)
-   I have been redeemed through God's grace (Eph 1:7)
-   I have received power through the Holy Spirit (Acts 1:8)
-   Jesus is always with me (Matt 28:20)
-   I am a new creation in Christ (2 Cor 5:17)
-   I am an ambassador for Christ (2 Cor 5:20)

For videos, resources, and tools:

MyNearDeathExperiment.com

CrossSection.com